Building Vision

Building Vision

A Constructivist-Developmental Approach to Spiritual Growth and Leadership

JEAN-PAUL GEDEON

INTRODUCTION BY JOYCE E. BELLOUS

WIPF & STOCK · Eugene, Oregon

BUILDING VISION
A Constructivist-Developmental Approach to Spiritual Growth and Leadership

Copyright © 2010 Jean-Paul Gedeon. All rights reserved. Except for brief quotations in critical publications or reviews, no part of this book may be reproduced in any manner without prior written permission from the publisher. Write: Permissions, Wipf and Stock Publishers, 199 W. 8th Ave., Suite 3, Eugene, OR 97401.

Wipf & Stock
An Imprint of Wipf and Stock Publishers
199 W. 8th Ave., Suite 3
Eugene, OR 97401
www.wipfandstock.com

ISBN 13: 978-1-60608-848-7

Manufactured in the U.S.A.

All scripture quotations, unless otherwise indicated, are taken from the Holy Bible, New International Version®, NIV®. Copyright ©1973, 1978, 1984 by Biblica, Inc.™ Used by permission of Zondervan. All rights reserved worldwide.

To Mikki and Chloe:
my deepest soul and my tenderest heart.

Contents

Preface ix
Acknowledgments xiii
Introduction by Joyce E. Bellous xv

SECTION ONE   VISION: THE CONSTRUCTIVIST-DEVELOPMENTAL FRAMEWORK OF SPIRITUAL GROWTH

Prologue 3

1 Epistemology 7

2 Defining Terms 17

3 The Theory of Growth 50

SECTION TWO   SEEING: THOUGHT AND ACTION IN SPIRITUAL LEADERSHIP

Prologue Revisited 93

4 The Goals of Spiritual Leadership 97

5 Creating Environment 127

6 Creating a Proper Attitude 146

7 Constructivist-Developmental Practices 156

Prologue Extended 173

Bibliography 177

Preface

MANY YEARS AGO, I sat down with some friends to watch a popular movie. It was one of those regular 'shoot-em-up', 'save-the-world', science-fiction type films that was garnering much popular and media acclaim. As I settled in and looked forward to be taken up into another world for a couple of hours, I was surprised to find that the experience did the exact opposite: it planted me firmly in the here-and-now, and got me thinking deeply about an issue that had been weighing on my mind. In the movie (as with all these movies), the Earth was in danger of being destroyed by some hostile (a rather ugly looking) alien force. In response, the whole of Earth's leadership convened to determine what course of action was appropriate, how to save all life on Earth. It was an intense and hard-hitting emotional scene, with much table banging, political subterfuge, and subtle posturing, as each member of the convened Council chimed in with theories and warnings. What struck me about this particular scene, however, was not the novel political structure of the futuristic, unified global government, nor the confounding vocabulary used in naming technological gadgets and unusual energy sources. Rather, what caught my attention was the attendance list of this crucial meeting.

In this moment, when the Earth's very existence was hanging in the balance, the 'President of Earth' convened a world-class team of political advisors, scientists, astronomers, military leaders, physicians, academics, and yes . . . Spiritual Leaders. I was astounded to see that, in the world of this movie, Spiritual Leaders were given the same regard and extended the same respect as their scientific and military counterpart, and in fact, were often given veto power over particular options. This veto power was not extended to Spiritual Leaders because they were somehow guardians of morality (quite the opposite—all characters at the table were equally concerned with their own brand of morality). Rather, this veto power was extended to them because they were perceived as experts *par excellence* in integrated human ontology.

And I began thinking: why is this striking me as so wonderfully novel? Is it because in today's society, Spiritual Leaders are not seen as useful members of Councils that would elucidate courses of action that are so pivotal for humankind? Is it because the war between Science and Faith has driven a deep wedge between the disciplines, such that Science is popularly viewed as reliable and unbiased, whereas Faith is often viewed with suspicion? Or is it simply because Spiritual Leaders do not have a reputation for being experts *par excellence* of human ontology?

In addition to these questions, my mind kept wandering: wouldn't it be wonderful if we could create a world in which Spiritual Leadership was regarded as highly as this movie was presenting? What would Spiritual Leadership have to do, then, to reverse the downward slide it is experiencing and begin climbing the mountain to a new, and more permanent cultural regard?

These are the founding questions that brought me to researching and writing this book.

While watching this movie, what I envisioned was a future in which a humble Spiritual Leadership was deeply valued by culture because of the depth and cogency of its insights, the sharpness of its perceptions, the empirical groundedness of its practices, the ecumenicalism of its inspiration, and the all-pervasive nature of its connectedness. In essence, what I envisioned was my deepest hope for my profession: that it realign itself to meet the considerable and daunting needs of post-modern culture and thereby gain ascendency as a premiere arena of mental, emotional, relational, and existential health. To a great degree, the promotion of this image has become a sort of calling for me, and these pages are written in the hopes of sparking a conversation that would move all Spiritual Leadership in this direction. Achieving such a vision, however, will not be a simple matter of garnering agreement from Leaders, counselors, and care-givers. Far from it. It is my belief that the move toward this wholistic and inspiring vision will only come through a fundamental and qualitative redefinition of what we perceive Spiritual Leadership to be, what we conceive of its goals to be, and what direction we feel it should take in the post-modern jumble of our current culture.

In short, this book is proposing a model of engagement that I believe closes the gap between the traditional messages of Christian Spiritual Leadership and the often unmet exigencies of our post-modern mindset. To that end, the following pages propose a particular method of engaging clients, and explain both the science and the theology behind that method. Thus, this work focuses on the general topic of transformative Spiritual Leadership as seen through a constructivist-developmental lens. Part 1 of the book is dedicated to the psychological and philosophical elucidation of this model of engagement, as well as to the explication of its theological underpinnings. Part 2 applies the tenets introduced in Part 1, and proposes dimensions of care necessary for the development of growthful and prayerful post-modern therapeutic environments. As such, this work is not a treatise on the detailed, internal, and swirling complexity of a psychological and theological school of thought. Rather, it is meant to act as an introduction of two established fields to one another: constructivist-developmentalism and pastoral care/counseling.

To that end, the following pages are meant to encourage a larger scholarly discussion around useful, post-modern formats of engagement for Spiritual Leaders—formats that would position Spiritual Leadership to gain further spiritual depth as well as cultural regard, existential honesty as well as scientific relevance, inter-discipline engagement as well as widespread epistemological prominence. These pages are also meant to sound a respectful challenge to the status quo of Spiritual Leadership. In short, the intention of the following pages is to act as a transformative voice in pastoral care culture—a voice that believes in ecumenical synergy, in universal respect, and in the deep-seated confidence required of a holy Spiritual Leadership taking on a post-modern world of entitlement and globalism. Only by meeting our post-modern care seekers and clients in the way they need to be met can we hope to walk with them through the vagaries of spiritual growth and transformation. Only by meeting care seekers and clients in the proclivities of their internal cultures can Spiritual leadership hope to remain cogent in this shifting world. Only through holding the unique exigencies of each care seeker within a culture of groundedness and spiritual centeredness can we hope to reflect the Christ-like love demanded for spiritual transformation. And only through the diligent care of each care-seeker and a truly novel and growthful orientation toward the integrated promotion of spirituality, can Spiritual Leadership hope to garner the generalized respect it deserves to be seen as an indispensible component of humanity's health around the world. Hence, the purpose of the following pages is to propose a framework of engagement, of spiritual maturity, and of transformative impetus that I believe would promote this fine vision of Spiritual Leadership in our difficult, global, and post-modern world.

Jean-Paul Gedeon
February 2010

Acknowledgments

This work would not have been possible without the belief and encouragement of three very important people:

I am deeply grateful to my mentor Joyce Bellous for her commitment to my vision in this endeavor. Joyce has gone out of her way to express belief in and encouragement for my explorations and growth. In times of personal fatigue and inevitable lethargy, her unwavering positivity and gentle empathy helped me find the drive I needed to push forward. Joyce, I thank you from the bottom of my heart! I look forward to many more discoveries and laughs in the future.

I would also like to acknowledge the guidance of Mark Boda. To me, Mark was a receptive, accepting, and interested fellow in the development of this work. Mark, for your patience, insight, and wonderful sense of humor, I thank you.

Finally, I would like to thank my wife Julia. In these years of frenetic happenings, Julia has stood beside me in staggering fortitude and generosity. With an open heart and loving kindness, she patiently took care of many daily details in order to allow me to cloister myself, writing and researching. For acting as friend, supporter, encourager, editor, mirror, and advocate, I am deeply grateful. As always, I more clearly learn how to see God's face because of your influence in my life.

Introduction

Growing old isn't the same as growing up. Human maturity is hard won. In a society that sells so many products, places and opportunities for adults only, one wonders what people hope for as they make these purchases. What do consumers think will make life good? In our big box world of purchasing power, we buy things to make us look and feel young. Being old is as welcome as the plague. Unfortunately, maturity seems to have gone missing along with the pursuit of youthfulness. In particular, being mature is unattractive because it generally requires us to set limits on what we want, or believe we need for ourselves, and what we're willing to pay to secure our self-interests. The attention we pay to ourselves is often at the expense of those who depend on us.

It's not a simple question of staying away from shopping centers. We believe our buying power props up the economy. We're committed to consuming, just as Henry Ford taught us to be.[1] The last century got its grounding on the idea that consumerism is healthy for the economy in general and families in particular. We feel obliged to purchase; we've come to believe it's the way to hold society together. And much of our economy depends on the consumption of goods. We feel torn: we suspect we shouldn't buy so much, but we're afraid to stop. Endlessly consuming has a tendency to draw us away from self-sacrifice, and places more emphasis on buying things for people we love than being with them. But decrying consumerism is old hat. Everyone is against consumerism, at least in theory. What should we do about the discomfort we feel? Consumerism, 'me-ism', is so powerful that we're numb to the next step. How do we move out of the present moment into a space that's more relational, more relaxed, and less materialistic?

For those questions, this book is timely, especially for those engaged in pastoral care and pastoral counseling. Its timeliness moves in

---

1. Steven Watts, *The People's Tycoon: Henry Ford and the American century.* New York: Vintage Books, 2006.

two directions. It's a book *of* and a book *for* the present moment. It's a book of our times because it's situated within a pressing social issue: everyone's need to communicate authentically with people they live and work with (those who are familiars and those who are strangers) to sustain healthy relationships with them. It's a book for our times because it stimulates the evolution of ordinary consciousness. The book *is* what it talks *about*. We're caught at a point in time when humanity, at least in the West, has to move forward if we're to find our way open to the future. It's a book for our times because it helps focus the project of becoming a mature spiritual person, and leader, by identifying the process and the point of growing up.

Mature believers accept that they have obligations to others and to God that ground the possibility of being in healthy relationships. Relationality is the developed ability to initiate, support, repair and sustain relationships with others, including God. The capacity to be in relationship has taken on new significance in the progress of human rights over the last few hundred years. As British social theorist Edward Milliband observed,

> the eighteenth century saw individuals granted civil rights (equality before the law), the nineteenth and early twentieth century brought political rights (equality of the franchise), and the early twentieth century onwards, [encouraged] social rights (based on principles of equal access to education, health care, housing, etc.)[2]

Miliband is not naive in describing human progress. He refers to developments in human rights as a rough and ready assessment of this period of history. Clearly, equality is not yet realized in multicultural environments. But the importance of his analysis for my purposes is to point out two implications that impact our capacity to be in relationship.

In addition to advancements Milliband outlined and during their development, other theorists recognized the need for humanity's material support since "the senses of human being can operate at a merely animal level—if they are not cultivated by appropriate education, by leisure for play and self-expression, by valuable associations with others"; American philosopher Martha Nussbaum added freedom of worship to this list.[3] Based on interactions with social theorist Amartya Sen, whose

---

2. Anthony Giddens and Patrick Diamond, (eds.), *The New Egalitarianism*. Cambridge: Polity Press, 2005, 40.

3. Martha Nussbaum, *Women and Human Development*. Cambridge: Cambridge

work with the United Nations has significant impact on promoting human rights globally, and by collaborating with African and Indian women in both countries, Nussbaum's analysis of human needs adds a further dimension.

Nussbaum's work implies a fundamental human need for relational resources so that all people may live a truly human life.[4] She's not alone in her assertion that we can't live truly human lives if we're caught in social conditions of relational poverty. In the current development of rights language, healthy relationships play a pivotal role. It's more essential to have healthy relationships, and for everyone to receive adequate attention from others, than to have lots of money. Relational support is felt primarily in adequate, appropriate attention from one's environment. Just as we can see who has wealth, social power, and value, discerning those with an ability to get and keep attention is a marker of social plenty in terms of human worth and privilege.[5] Getting adequate, appropriate attention is a central issue in becoming a spiritually mature person; the willingness and ability to give others adequate attention is a sign of maturity. The greatest gift we offer at the present moment, to ourselves and other people, is to give our full attention to what is meant in the attempts we make to communicate with one another.

Perhaps we feel successful at securing adequate attention for those we love, those who are near to us. But the times in which we live require more of our maturity than only looking after our own. Christianity has always required more of us than to merely love those who are like us and are easily able to meet our expectations and satisfy our needs. Relational support, for the mature, calls us to extend ourselves beyond the familiar. I suggest that the advantages of extending ourselves past taken-for-granted assumptions about the way the world is, and ought to be, will, in the long run, benefit our intimate relationships as well.

When I say Gedeon's book is for our times, I'm using a macro lens to magnify the moment in which we live by looking backward. In the West, the twentieth century moved through two socio-cultural-political phases characterized by the terms imperialism and relativism. These two

---

University Press, 2000, 72.

4. Martha Nussbaum, *Women and Human Development; Sex and Social Justice*. Oxford: Oxford University Press, 1999.

5. Charles Derber, *The Pursuit of Attention*. New York: Oxford University Press, 2000.

words worked on each other to move us toward a new possibility, one this book addresses directly. In the first decades of the last century, being white, free, and adult (21 years old) opened up a new era for men and women. The world belonged to them; yet that freedom encompassed a burden that many carried consciously. On an analysis from above (i.e., the point of view of privilege), their idea was that the whole world would be better if white, western, male values spread to all parts of the globe. That sentiment, the White Man's Burden, motivated cultural imperialism. Colonialism, characteristic of the period, left its indelible print on people groups who had not invited White Man's concern. They experienced it as an invasion that destroyed local culture and seemed more interested in taking their resources than refining their humanity. Imperialism has a long history that is typified by conquest and dehumanization.

An analysis of imperialism from below (i.e., from those who suffered it), opened the possibility of seeing imperialism for what it is—an unwelcome intrusion into another region, made possible by superior technology (e.g., weaponry), for the benefit of invaders and to the detriment of local peoples. That insight inspired privileged white Westerners to shift toward cultural relativism in reaction to the awareness of what went wrong. I don't suggest that the shift was pervasive or complete. Imperialism hasn't disappeared. However, the shock of looking at imperialism from below, from the perspective of men such as Franz Fanon, caused theorists to recoil from the taken-for-granted assumptions of superiority that were inherent in imperialism. Researchers began to value local culture. The insight developed into cultural relativism, the view that every culture has value and is true for its own sake, regardless of its differences from white, Western male (and generally) Christian culture. Relativism pervaded the West during the last half of the twentieth century, until it became a widely accepted, dominant view that drove us toward political correctness.

Relativism remains a strong cultural belief in North America and elsewhere even though it is unsustainable psychologically, politically and philosophically. No one can live by its premise that every view is of equal value and be psychologically well; some of our values take precedence over others or we remain confused and uncommitted. We stopped practising political relativism when the West used sanctions against countries that violated human rights within their own borders, as we did in response to Apartheid in South Africa.

Philosophically, relativism collapses in on itself. For example, if I were to write on a blackboard the statement, 'every view is of equal value' the next statement that I wrote would have to be as true as this first one. To say that statements that describe the world are of equal value is to claim that they describe the world equally accurately or 'truly'. Yet, if the second statement is, 'every view is not of equal value', which is a perfectly logical statement to make, the two statements on the board cancel each other out. If the first is true, the second can't be. If the second is true, the first one can't be. Relativism is most useful if it helps us see that people attach different meanings to life experiences. The problem that relativism presented to the last century was its failure to distinguish truth from meaning. This philosophical point is important psychologically. We're living in times of general confusion that creates deep-going personal and social harm.

On the positive side, the phase of relativism allowed theorists to get critical distance from their own settled worldviews, which had been used imperialistically. Critical reflection, that's so necessary to becoming a spiritually mature person, relies on seeing that there's more than one way to do things and more than one set of values. It also reveals that particular values are meaningful within their own framework, which is one of the insights that generated cultural relativism at its start. But here's the problem. Cultural relativism is a well-used intellectual tool when it pays attention to the way meaning is constructed and situated within a given context. It tells us a great deal about what someone means: it tells us very little about what is true. It's the shift to comprehending meaning first of all during a social interaction that this book helps us to perceive.

Relativism's most potent impact is that it allows us to see what we believe ourselves. Our beliefs, values, points of view are transparent to us until we realize that someone else sees the same issue differently. Suppose you move into a dorm and you have a stranger as a roommate. The first morning you're shocked to see her squeeze her toothpaste tube from the middle. You've always squeezed the tube from the end, slowly and meticulously. She grabs her toothpaste unceremoniously in the middle, and you disapprove. Prior to the experience of sharing a dorm room, you weren't conscious of your own toothpaste tube practice. It was just the way things were. You didn't know there was another way. Your initial reaction is negative. You're disturbed. She's doing it incorrectly. Then, finally, you realize that your relationship matters more than how she brushes her teeth. That shift takes time.

But a question crops up: How to apply toothpaste to *your* toothbrush so that you don't offend your roommate? You've never thought about it before and your options appear before you: Keep squeezing from the bottom and maybe she'll get the hint; lock the bathroom door when you're brushing your teeth; ignore what she's doing as if it weren't happening; accept that every way of squeezing toothpaste tubes is of equal value. But notice that the last option inevitably challenges your own meticulousness. It's hard to maintain a practice that you've prized in the past, while being relativistic about the practice in general. It would be very odd to stop brushing your teeth altogether (or do so twice a year, at Christmas and Easter) as a way to dissolve your dilemma. It would be ignored, not resolved. But suppose you rejected your own meticulousness outright and took on your roommate's approach. Surely it's evident that this would be a mere exchange and not a move forward. Yet this is what many Christians did in the last century as a way to be inoffensive to those who differed from them. In many places, we're too shy to be ourselves. We feel unsafe.

Relativism can draw us into conflict between theory and practice. As theory, it became, and still is, a poorly employed intellectual tool. It may move us to abandon our values. Improperly used, it disconnects us from others: we're locked inside the bathroom of 'our own truth' and locked outside any agreement about what really matters to all of us, as human beings. We flounder without core values. Imperialism and relativism are deeply isolating. In practice, it's abusive to be an imperialist and impossible to be a consistent relativist.

The usefulness of relativism, at macro and personal levels, is to break the hold that settled worldviews have on us. This isn't the same as discarding them. Rather it's an opportunity to rethink and revitalize them. Modern reformers (e.g., Freud) recommended rejecting our early worldviews, especially our belief in God, as a necessary step in growing up. In this, they were quite incorrect as to how worldviews function psychologically, socially and relationally in the construction of personal meaning. Freud had no excuse for arguing for the rejection option; his own theories posited that our initial concepts don't go away. They can be used, revised or repressed but they remain as an imprint of early experience, forming the foundation for accumulating meaning over time.[6]

---

6. Ana-Maria Rizzuto, *Why did Freud Reject God?* New Haven: Yale University Press 1998.

Relativism is not the final destination; it's a point along the way to becoming a mature person. In terms of spiritual maturity, the function of relativism is to help us realize that spirituality is about the formation of meaning, more than it's about truth, the whole truth and nothing but the truth that's embedded in the worldviews we form by early adolescence. White, western, male values are a legitimate way of looking at the world, but not the only way. The project of being in community with others and remaining true to ourselves requires us to consider the meaning we live by as a partial representation of the world. As scripture says, 'Now we see through a glass darkly; then we shall see face to face'.

This book shows how part of the evolution of ordinary consciousness moves through similar phases to the social movement from imperialism to relativism and beyond, to a third option. To grow up is to grasp what we think now, so we can decide whether we want to continue to rely on this way of perceiving the world, other people and God for the rest of our lives.

The break that relativism offers is as an antidote to imperialistic tendencies, but in reaction to its liberal lack of certainty, many find it necessary to reassert core religious or political values in a way often referred to as fundamentalism. They take the option of barricading themselves against the confusion that relativism creates. In terms of the macro-level process I'm describing, I think there's a better option, captured in social theorist Kwame Anthony Appiah's cosmopolitanism. As he put it,

> Each person you know about and can affect is someone to whom you have responsibilities: to say this is just to affirm the very idea of morality. The challenge, then, is to take minds and hearts formed over long millennia of living in local troops and equip them with ideas and institutions that will allow us to live together as the global tribe we have become.[7]

His cosmopolitanism is not relativism, multiculturalism or globalization. It has its center in two interwoven strands of thought: one of them is that we have obligations to others that stretch beyond kith, kin and citizenship; the second is that a sense of obligation isn't meant to neutralize the significance of particular people's values, beliefs and ways of life that are close to us.[8]

---

7. Kwame Anthony Appiah, *Cosmopolitanism: Ethics in a World of Strangers.* New York: W.W. Norton & Company, 2006, xiii.

8. *Cosmopolitanism*, xv.

Cosmopolitanism, as he stipulates the term, is a challenge that addresses our need to live together in local and global realities. What obligates us toward each other is the thread of humanity that unites the human tribe. His idea is congruent with Kant's moral framework. Kant thought that "obligation applies to all of us since the earth is round and connected. As a consequence, every part of the earth affects other parts and people cannot escape these effects without leaving the face of the earth."[9] To ground moral obligation, Kant made a model for humanity focused on male heads of households. Using gender exclusive language, he said that mankind has a duty to himself on the basis of the humanity within him *as a sensible being* and *as a free being*. In so saying, he shaped our idea of modern humanity. Kant constructed moral obligation on the bases of duty to oneself and to God's existence.[10]

Much of what motivated Kant grew out of his reading of Jean-Jacques Rousseau's work. For Rousseau, the overwhelming issue coming out of the breakdown of medieval social order and the rise of modernity was the troubling question of how we could learn to be ourselves while in relationship with other people. This book is a response to that core modern problem of linking authenticity (being ourselves) and integration (being with others). It affirms the scriptural truth that for humanity as a whole, knowledge is partial. Further, the book articulates limits to our freedom to focus entirely on ourselves that tends to characterize the West. Our refusal to accept these limits is a political problem as well as a spiritual one. As Zygmunt Bauman put it,

> The art of politics, if it happens to be democratic politics, is about dismantling the limits to citizens' freedom; but it is also about self-limitation: about making citizens free in order to enable them to set, individually and collectively, their own individual

---

9. Mary Gregor, (ed.), *Kant: Metaphysics of Morals.* Cambridge: Cambridge University Press, 1996, 50.

10. The spiritual implications of God's existence permit pure reason to flourish on its own terms as long as it doesn't forget its inherent needs. Hence to Kant, an individual was *not* free to pursue his own thinking wherever it might lead, an option he specifically rejected; extreme freedom destroys reason due to the violation of its own laws, i.e., needs. If reason prizes extreme freedom, a *felt* sense of obligation to human community is lost. See Immanuel Kant, "What does it mean to orient oneself in thinking?" in A. Wood and G. di Giovanni, *Kant: Religion Within the Boundaries of Mere Reason.* Cambridge: Cambridge University Press, 1998, 3–14.

and collective limits and that…point has been all but lost. [In the present social climate] all limits are off-limits.[11]

Mature people know they're not free to do whatever they like; they understand the value of self-limitation and hold good reasons for submitting themselves to it.

Gedeon is clear that the evolutionary process of maturity invites us to revisit the meanings we made when we were young as we interact with others. If we refuse to reconsider meanings made during the first phases of our lives, we build a fortress with them as a barricade to gathering more self and social knowledge. In the process of growing up, we are called on to reflect upon and revise our way of seeing the world in light of new evidence. That evidence arises from the reality of the other: we allow others to speak for themselves, including the Living God, who is more than we can capture in the settled worldview of an adolescent. We also hear ourselves in new ways. The good news is that there's a model for maturity in Paul's example.

In a remarkable passage of scripture, Paul conveys a level of spiritual maturity we seldom see in ourselves or in other believers. He unveils the maturity of his inmost being when he says:

> So then, you ought to regard us as servants of Christ and as those entrusted with the secret things of God. Now it is required that those who have been given a trust must prove faithful. I care very little if I am judged by you or by any human court; indeed, I do not even judge myself. My conscience is clear, but that does not make me innocent. It is the Lord who judges me. 1Cor. 4:1–4.[12]

The capacity Paul developed represents a high point in the meaning-making activity of an ordinary person who knows Jesus Christ exceptionally well. The outcome of his relationship with God is the freedom to be authentic in the company of others, even those who differ sharply with him. That freedom in Christ is the reward of maturity, a reward worth seeking with a whole heart. This book helps us toward that end.

Joyce E. Bellous

---

11. Zygmunt Bauman, *In Search of Politics*. Stanford: Stanford University Press, 1999, 4–5.

12. *The Holy Bible*, New International Version, Inclusive Language Edition. London: Hodder & Stoughton.

Section One

Vision: The Constructivist-Developmental Framework of Spiritual Growth

Prologue

*The Spirit is never at rest but always engaged
in an ever-progressive motion, in giving itself new form.*

—Hegel

SEEING: WE MIGHT SAY that the whole action of spiritual growth is contained in this deceptively simple word. The overarching focus of our entire discussion in the following pages will focus on the complexities of seeing better—of being more aware, of developing fuller consciousness, of growing spiritually. As I hope to demonstrate, this increase in vision—in spiritual growth—is a founding inheritance of the Judeo-Christian paradigm, and as such, is essential to humanity's journey toward maturity, integrity, and connectedness—toward greater differentiated autonomy and toward greater integrated unity. In addition, the journey toward greater consciousness is the founding tenet of an overwhelming majority of secular psychological and anthropological theories that receive popular acclaim. As such, the question of increased consciousness (or the evolution of vision to be more precise) is an elementary and foundational facet of humanity's state that crosses the chasm between the Science orientation (those who choose to believe that what is to be accepted is that which can be accessed empirically) and the Faith orientation (those who choose to believe that all answers are held within writings, traditions, and beliefs). Since the evolution of consciousness is a concept that involves and supersedes any single orientation, it is a transformative and transcendental human element. For this reason, I view the philosophical and spiritual history of humankind as the elaboration of an ever-more expansive awareness, an ever-more evolved consciousness, and an ever-more perfected vision, all within a wondrous and holy Creation where there is always something more to be seen.

But, at the base of greater vision is growth. Growth is costly. I believe that humanity is the whole that unfolds, the sacred consciousness that strives ever further, and the motion of evolution that risks the pangs of growth. The work in these pages is a respectful challenge to the status quo in Spiritual Leadership, and consequently asks its readers to risk these very pangs.

Growth is a paramount concept to me. As an educator and counselor, I have expended vast amounts of energy in the pursuit of the elucidation of the progression of human spiritual growth. I call myself an educator because I believe that I am called to disseminate this elucidation of growth throughout the field of Spiritual Leadership in order to challenge Leaders toward greater usefulness, reception, and compassion. I call myself a counselor because I believe that a powerful road to personal healing lies in the participation in, and cherishing of, compassionate inter- and intra-personal relationships. Consequently, I am writing this book in the hopes of raising a considered alternative to the more traditional concepts of Spiritual Leadership, as it is presented in the Judeo-Christian conception: can we redefine the role of Spiritual Leaders in order to develop and accept a founding epistemology that transcends and unites views and cultures that have traditionally pitted us against one another? Can we redefine the role for Spiritual Leaders in order to set the basis for a Christian culture that is built upon concern for each individual, and not concern for the propagation of a traditional system?

Through a consideration of both Science and Faith orientations, this book will propose a constructivist-developmental approach to spiritual growth and Spiritual Leadership. This approach bases itself on the personal integration of meaning, on the tenets of experiential learning, and on the wisdom of Biblical teachings. It is my hope that through this elucidation, our very conception of God will begin an evolution whereby it can grow into an image large enough to hold our collective challenges. It is also my hope that through investigations such as these, the substance and essence of Spiritual Leadership will be redefined and will evolve into a compassionate and holy repository, powerful enough to represent this awesome God.

As we move through the chapters, two concepts will be continuously juxtaposed: the concepts of substance and essence. For the purposes of this work, I will use these terms to denote specific and limited definitions. By 'substance', I will refer to those elements of the framework that are based in investigation, elucidation, and human study. By 'essence', I will refer to those elements of the framework that are based in soulfulness, wisdom, and spiritual teaching. It is my belief that a combination of these two fields brings us closer to a full act of knowing—biased to neither the Science orientation nor the Faith orientation. In order to proceed to a truthful and innocent redefinition of Spiritual Leadership, I do not believe we can exonerate ourselves from the complexities and difficulties of intellectual and spiritual honesty. As such, substance and essence will be presented as two sides of the 'awareness' coin.

But awareness of what? What are the arguments presented in the chapters ahead? There are two:

1. Human growth is an evolution of consciousness which gives rise to spirituality and thus, the personal levels of thought, affect, and relationship. This 'ground' is the founding element of meaning-constitutive consciousness. Evolution takes place through a process of Emergence of ever-increasing forms of complexity within a person's internal equilibrium. This evolution is inherent in the Judeo-Christian inheritance and is illuminated by the Pentateuchal narrative.

2. Spiritual Leaders humbly accompany clients through the process of Emergence by co-constructing with the client a culture of embeddedness.[1] This culture involves goal orientation, environment-creation, attitudinal alignment, and practical techniques. The culture is created through an unwavering commitment of the Spiritual Leader to the person of the client and not through a staunch defense of the system within which the Spiritual Leader functions.

These are complex statements to be sure—but, it is the purpose of this work to parse out the pieces of these arguments and present them in cogent chunks. In the pages ahead, I will investigate the above arguments through a theologized psychology where the study of psychology is taken in its literal sense: studying *psyche* and studying *logos*. It is my firm belief that the evolution of *psyche* and the progression of *logos* are the seminal factors in an 'ever-progressive motion' of the spirit. In asking about the difficult issues inherent in being human, our approach to psychology is a true scrutiny of the ability to more fully see.

1. I am indebted to Robert Kegan for this term. For more on cultures of embeddedness, please see, Kegan, *Evolving Self, In Over Our Heads*.

1

Epistemology

SUBSTANCE: SCIENCE AND FAITH—A FULL ACT OF KNOWLEDGE

AT FIRST BLUSH, IT appears as though the modern world was born of an anti-religious movement: humanity becoming self-sufficient and reason supplanting the supremacy of belief.[1] In our generation, we are constantly bombarded by talk of the conflict between Science and Faith, between Creation and Empiricism, between the measurable and the mysterious. As the realm of Science found its grounding and began to prove itself as a leading force in the improvement of the human condition, it achieved ascendency, gaining strong epistemological currency throughout many of the most prominent cultures in the world. In fact, it began to appear as a foregone conclusion that Science was destined to take the place of Faith as the founding epistemology of human engagement. So intense is this struggle for the prestige of influence that cultural attitudes have begun to view Science and Faith as antonyms of one another. But, as the tension is prolonged, a resolution, in which one of these warring factions is discredited as nonsense and the other acclaimed as authoritative, has begun to fade as a viable possibility. There will never be a world in which the biases of any one of these two factions will find authoritative and accepted supremacy over the epistemology of the human race. I believe, therefore, that this conflict seems to demand a resolution in terms of an entirely different form of balance—not in elimination and duality, but rather in synergistic synthesis. The purpose of this section is to set out the founding epistemological framework through which I have approached my investigation of spiritual growth: the epistemology

---

1. Erickson, *Childhood and Society,* 256.

of synthesis between Science and Faith. It is only through this kind of phenomenology that I believe the inescapable Internal aspects of God's Creation as well as the undeniable External aspects of the empirical Universe will be taken into account in elucidating spiritual formation.

So far as I understand it, the quarrel between Science and Faith depends not on an impossibility of integrating both types of knowledge into a coherent whole, but rather on the difficulty of the two schools in finding harmonious integration, and balanced dialogue. On the one hand, the Scientific orientation insists on talking about objects solely as empirically perceivable, quantitatively apprehendable, external actions and mechanistic relationships—as if humanity could somehow stand apart from its observations and propound a sort of purely objective account of phenomena. On the other hand, the Faith orientation is just as obstinately determined to introspectively stipulate that objects are nothing other than immanent workings of the Divine—as if empirical measurements, observations, and findings are somehow shallow, illusory, misleading, or even deceitful. Fueled by almost two centuries of struggle, neither side has effectively succeeded in discrediting its adversary. They fight in fundamentally different dimensions and as such are unable to answer each other's queries. It is the fragmented and compartmentalized vision of these factions that leads me to invest my conviction in the realm of unity and synthesis.

In my opinion, a synthesis of the Science and Faith orientations results in the only viable act of knowing that is comprehensive enough to encompass the complexities of spiritual growth. The strength of this growth lies in its ability to address aspects of observation, investigation, and reason, while equally paying heed to the elements of inspiration, intuition, and belief. As such, the framework allows the faithful to inform the scientific and the scientific to inform the faithful—whereby each discipline is both a rich source of questions as well as a wise and penetrating source of answers to the complexities of our lived experiences. It is through this dialectical form of awareness, rather than through the traditional, dualistic form, that I believe humanity comes closer to apprehending a complete act of knowing. God has revealed Himself to humanity both through Creation (Science orientation) and through Scripture (Faith orientation). Just as an artist cannot create a work without infusing it with his unique creative imprint, so Creation could not exist devoid of the transcendental dimensions of Holiness. Thus, neither in its mission nor its achievements can Science go to its limits without becoming tinged in mysticism and charged with faith. For example, I am particularly struck by the many scientific accounts of the complexities and characteristics of DNA—the very building blocks of our genetic material. Throughout the literature dealing with this fascinating topic, narratives seem to move more and more from a discussion of base pairs, sugar-phosphate backbones, and 'lock-and-key' protein coding structures, to spiritual discussions of the staggering unity that infuses all living beings on Earth. As such, the scientific discussion of DNA very often leads to a grasping of a seminal, universal, and basic connectedness of all living things to other living things—regardless of species denotation, geographical localities, or temporal locations.

On the other side of the coin, just as a composer's temperament is betrayed by the timbre, intensity, and force of his composition, so devotion could not exist devoid of insight into the complexity, beauty, and perfection of the observed world. After all, the basis of allegory, illustration, metaphor, beauty, and interconnectedness is rooted in the empirically known vagaries of Nature itself. Hence, neither in its drive nor in its inspiration can Faith go to its limits without finding root and revelation in the actuality of the empirical universe. As such, Science finds fulfillment in Faith just as Faith finds fulfillment in Science. The disciplines, when viewed in this light, are promoted to the status of integrated and confluent phases of knowing, rather than dueling and contradictory sources of information. But not only do these disciplines flow into one another, they also interlink seamlessly, to those who choose to perceive it, as two faces of a knowledge coin.

I believe that, in the realm of Science, humanity will only continue to evolve, to work, to research, to expand, so long as it is prompted by a passionate drive. This drive is entirely dependent on the conviction, ironically non-demonstrable by Science, that the universe has some form of order and reversible perfection (a quantifiable faultlessness that can be inverted, understood, and predicted with flawless accuracy. In fact, reproduceability is one of the founding tenets of the scientific method). Equally ironically, it is in the passionate pursuit of this perfection that humanity engages in the faith-filled and seminal concept of 'progress'.[2]

---

2. In this context, I am referring to the popular notion of progress, which I define as the advancement of the state of the art of the scientific field, in order to enhance the quality of life of all human beings. In many scientific circles, this notion of progress

In addition, we can scientifically envisage an almost indefinite improvement in the human organism and in human society. As soon as we conceive of this perfected vision, however, we come face to face with the notion that this putative perfection would speak to all humankind everywhere. For example, we do not speak of seminal scientific discoveries as benefiting human beings living in, say, India exclusively. Rather, we are always keenly aware that all forward movement in the empirical world has ramifications for and a concrete hand in the progression of all humanity, regardless of its local incarnation or preliminary reason for investigation. Interestingly, the perfected and progressive world that we find described in the works of many scientific leaders is a world meant to benefit and fulfill all of humanity. Nowhere in the works of these brilliant thinkers do we find an extensive anthropological study of the needs of human beings across several cultures and continents. Instead, the scientific culture presumes that its findings are seminal and welcomed by all human beings, everywhere.

According to Teilhard de Chardin, the source of this perceived universal harmony could be nothing else than a super-rational intuition within each of us.[3] As such, can we truly say that scientific progress is somehow predicated on fundamental faith-filled tenets—those of universalism, connectedness, growth, and altruism? According to de Chardin, this is precisely the case. Therefore, from the scientific belief in reversible and empirical perfection, we arrive at the Faith-oriented belief in unity—conceived, intuited, but never measured. Furthermore, if we stipulate and reinforce the optimistic notions held within a framework of unity, we are pushed further along by the necessity of discovery—a necessity which fuels the impetus to push forward, to evolve, and to develop. Thus, it is my observation that as soon as Science outgrows its procedural and analytical investigations, it passes onto an epistemology of synthesis. This synthesis naturally culminates in the realization of some superior state of humanity, which in its very nature reintegrates and renews those very faithful forces against which it claims to be fighting. Therefore, I believe that Science and Faith are two conjugated phases and faces of one and the same complete and interlacing act of knowledge. This is the only act of knowledge that can embrace the past

---

finds expression in quasi-utopian, almost mystical conceptions of human health and culture.

3. de Chardin, *The Phenomenon of Man*, 79.

and the future of human evolution so as to contemplate, measure, and transcend both the observed and the believed. It is in the mutual reinforcement of the powers of Science and Faith, in the conjunction of reason and mysticism, that I believe the human spirit is destined to find the utmost degree of evolution, with the maximum thrust of its vital and holy force.

It is with eyes firmly fixed on the union of the External with the Internal, of the Scientific with the Faithful, that I proceed in the discussion of the complexities of spiritual growth from a constructivist-developmental viewpoint.

ESSENCE: STORY—A FULL ACT OF COMPREHENSION

Throughout the world of Biblical study, many distinct intellectual cultures have contributed their unique brand of information to the challenge of Scriptural interpretation: source analysts, redaction analysts, systematic theologians, linguistic scholars, historians, anthropologists, among many others. With all the various methodologies of approaching Scripture, it is no surprise that many readers of scholarly commentary find themselves confounded and confused by the complexity and intricacy presented in the interrelation of these different paths of study: an unfortunate happenstance. My approach will engage in a different yet emerging interpretational culture: the theology of narrative—an approach that, I believe, provides a much simpler, yet much more comprehensive apprehension of Biblical lessons and wisdom. In this section, I will outline my approach to the Biblical text, and delineate a narrative component that I consider to be paramount: story. But first, I must define what exactly I mean by a narrative approach to Scripture.

By 'narrative', I am referring to the body and form of the Biblical text *as we now have it*—in its complete form. It is the shape of this body, and the interrelations within it, to which I will appeal in my description of the Biblical roots of the constructivist-developmental framework. In other words, my approach to Scripture is to view the text as a completed whole, designed and guided by an over-arching intelligence, within which lies a thematic integrity. This integrity is rich enough to not only inform us of God's revelation to humanity, but also to allow us a glimpse into the transformation and evolution of humanity itself. As such, in concert with David Clines, I will deliberately steer away from two pervasive elements in Biblical analysis: atomism and geneticism.[4]

As Clines states, the tendency toward atomism is amply revealed by the content found in the pages of the proverbial scholarly journal. We are no longer surprised by the existence of vast articles written to explain the meaning and origin of a single word found in a particular Scriptural passage.[5] Nor are we amazed to encounter great scholarly energy devoted to the elucidation of the complexities of a minor detail within the Biblical narrative.

I recall several years ago, I engaged in a conversation with a colleague (I will call him Jason) about the nuances held within the complexities of Biblical Greek grammar. I remember sitting fascinated as Jason extolled for me a theory he had been researching over the course of the past few years. This theory involved the elucidation of a novel interpretation for the use of verbs in Biblical Greek. Jason was stipulating the wonders of viewing Greek tenses as aspectual rather than as temporal. As such, he believed that the present tense implied an immediacy and strong emphasis, whereas other verb tenses implied less dramatic emphases (for example, the past tense, he said, was used as the regular verb-of-choice in everyday discourse, and therefore held no special or particular emphasis beyond the lexical meaning of the word). He further intrigued me by translating certain verses he was working on using this new approach. On the page, he wrote the present-tense verbs in oversized, capital, red letters, the imperfect verbs in slightly less over-sized green letters, and the past-tense verbs, written in the same scale as the remainder of the text, in dark blue. He then asked me to read the verse raising or lowering my voice dramatically depending on the relative size and color of the words he had written down. I did so (ignoring the odd stares I received from the other patrons in the coffee shop), and to my extreme surprise, found that the verse did in fact change slightly in the presenting meaning and articulation. I was intrigued to hear more, and, in particular, to find out what this difference in grammatical emphasis meant for the greater Biblical message. Although he could walk me through the retranslation of many of my favorite verses using this new grammatical convention, Jason sadly and humbly admitted to me that he was unable

---

4. Clines, *The Theme of the Pentateuch*, 7.
5. Clines, *The Theme of the Pentateuch*, 7.

to elucidate the overarching effect such an approach would have on the New Testament, as well as on ministerial approaches in general.

After this particular encounter, I was struck by a very sobering thought: although this stream of study can provide a unique insight into a fuller appreciation of the nuances and historical accuracy of particular texts as written, it leaves out what I believe (in agreement with Clines) to be a paramount aspect of Biblical interpretation: personal, significant, and repeated engagement with the text.[6] It is not only through the challenge introduced by critics and scholarly insight, but also through the illumination effected by our personal experience, the need brought about by our personal struggles, the lacks branded into our beings by our inescapable fallenness, the hopes that crown our very dreams, that we come to construct and accept an understanding of the textual source before us. As such, Jason's research, as illuminating and enriching as it was to me, shared the fate of other atomic forms of study: by focusing solely on the minute and fascinating, it left unattended the personal, the soulful, and the integrated. As we shall see later, a personal and integrated construction of understanding is a founding principle in human consciousness and evolution as conceived through the constructivist-developmental framework. Throughout this book therefore, I will outline Biblical lessons that I have gleaned, not only from rounds of careful study (for which I am indebted to brilliant scholars such as Jason), but also from a repeated and prayerful personal engagement with the intricacies and morals contained within the entire Pentateuch. Therefore, as a parallel to the wholistic approach described above in the section about Science and Faith, I approach the text of the Bible with the same degree of wholism.

The second tendency found in Biblical analysis is that of geneticism. Geneticism is defined as the practice of reducing a particular investigation to an elucidation of the origins of an entity or stimulus. Geneticism is a very common practice in modern counseling and psychotherapy. We are forever being presented with images of the stereotyped therapist working with his or her client to uncover the primary and seminal source of an emotional, relational, or spiritual disturbance. The underlying belief of such practices seems to be that, by naming the origins of the presenting emotional disturbance, a degree of control and power is reclaimed by the naming agent (usually, the care seeker) over the disturbance. These practices, however, although they afford seekers a degree of

---

6. Clines, *The Theme of the Pentateuch*, 9.

self-efficacy and a great deal of personal insight, do not always provide direction as to the required intervention to rectify the disturbance in the future. After all, knowing how something came to exist does not always allow us to determine the best way to break future dispositional cycles related to it. As such, genetic approaches to counseling and therapy are usually not enough, in themselves. They often have to be coupled with forward-thinking interventions—interventions directed to the complexities of the here-and-now, the realities of today's habits as well as to the intentional breaking of those habits for a healthier tomorrow.

Similarly, when referring specifically to Biblical scholarship, by 'geneticism', I am referring to Clines' notion of the practice of reducing Biblical scholarship to a study of the origins and development of the extant Biblical texts and to the individual sources found compiled within a single narrative. Clines believes that a particular view of the nature of knowledge is promoted by the practice of geneticism: the belief that a text is best understood when its sources are reconstructed and its pre-history determined. In Old Testament studies, however, the sources and pre-history of the given text are mostly hypothetically determined.[7] Consequently, I believe that we are prudent to rely more heavily on the art that is Scriptural narrative, and concentrate on the wisdom imparted by its various articulations in its present form. In other words, although I do not decry or denigrate the scientific necessity of geneticism in Biblical scholarship, I am wary of awarding it the dominance often found in traditional circles. I believe that increased wisdom and knowledge of God, and not the reconstruction of original texts, is the primary focus of responsible exegesis. There is no doubt in my mind that the Biblical narrative is not to be taken solely as a conglomeration of individual accounts. Rather, I believe that it is best understood as a whole work, a constant train of thought emanating from an overarching Mind. After all, the whole is always so much more that simply the sum of the parts! And this tenet is true as much for biological systems as it is for the Pentateuch.

The Pentateuch is, to my mind, an outstanding example, within world literature, of the power, salience, and self-renewing function of the religious story. As such, scholars such as Thomas Mann suggest that it could serve as the paradigm for the interpretation of the bulk of Biblical material—story, and not history, serving as the primary mode of

---

7. Clines, *The Theme of the Pentateuch*, 9.

communication for religious truth.[8] To understand how the Pentateuch functions as a theological work that transcends its own time, I believe that we need to briefly explore the nature of story.

What is offered in a story is a world—imaginary or real, familiar or unfamiliar. To the degree that the reader of a story is imaginatively grasped by the story's spell, he or she enters the world of the narrative. We have all been privy to interactions with a great story in which the narrative grasps us with such force that it compels us to read voraciously, compulsively driving us to learn the fate of a particular character. Hence, the reader of such a story, when powerfully affected by it, becomes a willing participant in its world. Through increased familiarity with the story, the reader typically learns his or her way around the narrative world, until, to a significant degree, the reader takes it on as his or her own. The Pentateuch, then, performs a function of creating a world that is unlike that of its reader, and thus invites the reader to allow the limits and his or her own world to merge with those presented in the narrative. And it is here that we arrive at the crowning moment of the effect of the religious story: I believe that to respond to the invitation of entering another world is to allow oneself to be worked upon and influenced by the intricacies of that new world. That is, a reader exposes himself or herself to the possibility of the story coming into intimate dialogue with his or her own story. In this way, Biblical truths and lessons are considered and internalized by the reader. Spiritual perspectives are explored and spiritual intelligence is fostered.

As far as the Torah is concerned, this primary effect of story means that the narrative functions as a reality from beginning to end. No awkward historical question about the specific material of Torah can stand in the way of its narrative efficacy in creating a world, or in drawing its readers into participating in its world. Given half the degree of suspension of disbelief that we exercise everyday when we settle in front of a television screen, the reader of the Pentateuch soon comes to know the character of life lived in the tension between a promise given and a promise fulfilled, and the nature of action that is, at one and the same time, freely chosen and divinely inspired. In short, the reader comes face-to-face, within the constructed reality of his or her experiences, with the revelation of God and of self-transformation, as presented by the founding texts of the Old Testament.

8. Mann, *The Book of Torah*, 102.

My method in this book will be to approach the Old Testament account through the lens of narrative theology. Due to what I perceive to be the powerful gifts of the medium of story, I believe that this wholistic and comprehensive approach to Biblical interpretation is not only deeply relevant to our personal spiritual formation, but also in harmony with the general philosophy of synthesis through which I will approach the elucidation of constructivist-developmental spiritual growth.

2

Defining Terms

*The chief virtue that language can have is clearness,
and nothing detracts from it so much as the use of unfamiliar words.*

—HIPPOCRATES

SEVERAL YEARS AGO, WHILE conducting research on the vagaries of personal reasoning and epistemology, I found myself confounded—lost in a world of unfamiliar verbage, and drowning in a vortex of obscure linguistic conventions. Slowly over the course of several months of reading, I became acclimatized to this academic dialect and came to find my bearings in the subject area. It was as a result of that experience that I came to deeply appreciate Hippocrates' words—an appreciation that led me to the conviction of ensuring that my readers felt at ease with my choice of terminology. As such, the purpose of this chapter is to define terms that are fundamental to the elucidation of the constructivist-developmental framework of spiritual growth. In my desire to keep from using 'unfamiliar words', I have chosen terms that are commonly used in everyday contexts. Throughout this work, however, my application of the meaning of these words is specific.

1. SPIRITUALITY

Substance: Redefining Spirituality

There are few concepts more familiar than that of 'spirituality', and few that are as opaque. The nature of this inner power is so intangible that the whole scientific description of the physical universe can proceed without making a single mention of it.¹ Since there is little doubt that a significant proportion of our existence is grounded in the physical universe, I believe that nowhere is the need more urgent of bridging the Scientific and the Faithful than in the arena of our individual and collective pursuits of spirituality. Thus, the nature of this ephemeral term will finally find root in the empirical world while retaining its ascendancy in the inspirational. It will therefore span the totality of our human ontology. De Chardin said that there is a single energy operating throughout Creation, an energy through which the External/Objective, along with the Internal/Subjective hold together in a complementary counter-balance. It is an overarching energy that is at once a part of and greater than all the currently measurable and observable energies humanity can perceive. This energy, he christens 'spiritual energy'.² De Chardin believes that the human spirit is a focal point for this energy, effecting transformation in which the External and the Internal are integrated as beauty and truth.³ In agreement with de Chardin's inclusive and integrated stance, my definition of spirituality, which is relevant to the context of the constructivist-developmental framework, roots this otherwise celestial term into the reality of everyday growth.

To my mind, spirituality is a dynamic state of consciousness concerned with life's meaning and coherence. Thus, spirituality, the essence of spiritual energy, is a focused and overarching aspect of humanity that reaches into every level and dimension of human life, promoting development and awareness—bridging the mundane and the transcendent, the Scientific and the Faithful, the motivational and the inspirational. Spirituality is therefore a characteristic of the whole self (both internal and external) and not of an institutionalized practice or entity. Consequently, spirituality, as I interpret it, is not necessarily religious in its content or context.

In the 1950s, Paul Tillich published two of his classic works: *Dynamics of Faith* and *The Courage to Be*. These works dared to propose a conception of spirituality that transcended the traditional lines of organized religious groupings, histories, cultures, and rituals. In fact,

---

1. de Chardin, *The Phenomenon pf Man*, 27. de Chardin provides an excellent synthesized account of the confluence of astronomical and biological evolution with idealized spiritual development.

2. de Chardin, *The Phenomenon of Man*, 63.

3. de Chardin, *The Phenomenon of Man*, 68.

Tillich's notions moved spiritual discourse into the post-modern world by positing a degree of deep relativism to spiritual direction. According to Tillich, that which acted as a central drive to all spiritual action was that which grounded personal desire, need, and belief. In other words, that in which we put our faith (whether it be transcendent or mundane), that which we believe subtends personal meaning (whether compassionate or utilitarian), that to which we direct our meaning-constitutive energy and attention (whether individual or institutional) is the very thing that becomes the Ultimate in our conceptions of life's condition. Through his thorough and refreshingly honest probing, he stipulated that spirituality develops and forms as we assimilate experiences of trust and fidelity, mistrust and betrayal, with those closest to us (a conclusion reminiscent of Erik Erikson's work on epigenetic stages of development).[4] In addition, this Ultimate comes to act as a container for our pursuit of the greatest, most mysterious, and existentially worrying questions in our lives. As such, Tillich concludes that spirituality, at all levels, is the search for an overarching, integrating, and grounding trust, sufficiently cogent to give our lives unity and meaning.

Robert Fowler, working in a Tillichean mode, calls these values 'God values' because they concern and affect humanity as it turns its attention to the Ultimate (whatever an individual conceives the Ultimate to be). According to this view, our true worship, our real devotion directs itself toward the objects of our ultimate concerns.[5] These concerns formulate the driving force of our impetus to grow, to expand, and to discover, and are therefore much more dynamic and encompassing than claimed beliefs in a creed (Faith) or a set of doctoral propositions (Science).

Fowler supports his assertions by summarizing Wilfred Smith. Smith makes a seminal distinction between religion and spirituality. Speaking of religions as cumulative traditions, he suggests that we see these traditions as the speckled expressions of the beliefs of our forerunners. These cumulative traditions may constitute texts of Scripture and Law, including narratives, myths, prophecies, and revelations. In addition, they may involve symbols, oral traditions, rituals, music, dance, ethical teachings, creeds, historical accounts, and architecture, among innumerable other cultural expressions. I agree with Smith that these aspects create a living cumulative tradition that comes to address a certain group of contempo-

4. Erikson, *Childhood and Society*.
5. Fowler, *Stages of Faith*, 4.

rary people, at certain times and in certain places, and becomes for them a worldly grounding that awakens individual faith.[6] This point, however, drives home the difference between religion and my conception of spirituality. As a dynamic state of consciousness concerned with meaning and coherence, spirituality surpasses the often impersonal and moralizing cultures of cumulative traditions. Spirituality so defined presupposes life and drive—a consciousness, steeped in dynamism and movement, reaching for and assimilating the complexities and challenges of everyday life. Consequently, whereas religion is often seen as a traditional construct of prescription, spirituality is a personal, wholistic, and active mode of knowing, of composing, and of conceiving of life.

Care must be taken here, however. This is not to say that spirituality has no relation to religion. On the contrary, I believe that spirituality and religion are involved in a deeply reciprocal relationship. Each is active. Each grows and is renewed through its interaction with the other. Spirituality is awakened and nurtured by the elements of religious tradition, which inform, expand and deepen spiritual expression by providing a repertoire of mystery and inspiration. At the same time, religious tradition gains fresh vitality by being moulded into an expression of the spirituality of its adherents—an expression that breaks open barriers and brings life's experiences and practical apprehensions into the religious sphere.[7] One caveat stands, however: this account represents an ideal. It represents the interaction of spirituality and religion as it occurs only under ideal circumstances.

Spirituality, then, is a "deep, rich, and personal quality of human living. It is engendered by religious tradition, but it is a quality of the whole person. It is an orientation of personality, to one's Self, to one's neighbor, to the empirical universe, to God's creation; it is a total response."[8] It is a way of seeing what is perceived and of handling what is grasped. It is the capacity to live in more than a simple and mundane world. It is the developed capacity to see: to be aware of and act through the transcendent

---

6. Smith in Fowler, *Stages of Faith*, 9; Smith, *Belief and History*, chs. 6–7.

7. Fowler, *Stages of Faith*, 9.

8. Fowler, *Stages of Faith*, 11. In this definition, Fowler is defining his conception of 'faith'. Although my conception of spirituality is very different from Fowler's 'faith', they share many of the same properties, as well as the same fundamental impetus—the promotion of humanity's spiritual health.

dimension, while fostering the ability to connect with the experiential dimension. It is a being, a doing, a knowing, and a connecting.

I believe that we commit to a transcendent dimension because we individually judge that it contains clarity of direction, social centeredness, a scope large enough to contain our existential fears, and a grounded value system that can guide our progress. By committing ourselves to questing for that dimension, we develop a deep and personal sense of signification, direction, and meaning. Thus, to quote Fowler: "In a world of powerful forces that have an impact upon us, enlarging and diminishing us, forming and destroying us, we invest loyalty in and seek to align ourselves with those powers that sustain our lives and undergird our being."[9] The centers of power that are 'God values' for us, therefore, are those that confer meaning and worth upon each of us, and promise to sustain us in an otherwise dangerous and tiresome epistemological and existential culture. Spirituality, therefore, can be defined as a person's way of finding coherence in and giving meaning to the multiple forces that influence his or her life, along with a way of seeing and relating to others against the background of these forces. Thus, we return to Tillich's stipulation that spirituality is the relationship to that which orients us to the Ultimate.

Spirituality, then, is a verb—it is active, moving, and alive. We dynamically construct our consciousness from our experiences, from our forming and transforming of the seminal relationships in our lives, and from the development of the reciprocity we foster with each other and with the Ultimate. As such, spirituality is constantly evolving. It is, to my mind, the most fundamental category of the human struggle for a relationship with the transcendent aspects of life as well as a connection to the beauty and necessity of the mundane. Only through such a comprehensive relationship can human beings hope to nurture and evolve a greater sense of meaning and coherence in their lives—to approach Erikson's highest stages of Wisdom and Integrity.[10] The conception of spirituality as a state of consciousness implies that it involves an alignment of the will, which functions in harmony with a vision of one's ultimate concerns. It is, therefore, a universal feature of human living and human ontology. It is not a separate dimension of life, a compart-

---

9. Fowler, *Stages of Faith*, 21.
10. Erikson, *Childhood and Society*.

mentalized specialty. In the words of de Chardin, "[It] is the element of cosmic synthesis."[11]

Looking at spirituality through a constructivist-developmental lens reveals that the study of spirituality focuses on the way apprehension is constructed and structured as it gives form to the content of knowledge. In other words, spirituality allows us to investigate *how* a person knows (an universal concept) rather than *what* a person knows (an individual construct). As such, we can focus on the universal features of spirituality despite the variety of particular themes, symbols, and images that can be expressed. Furthermore, the constructivist-developmental view of spirituality stipulates a commitment to take seriously the fact that our previous choices of action and decision, our choices of images and stories, and our commitment to social communities together function to shape our consciousness. I believe that spirituality, so conceived, is a generalizable notion: one that is neither solely communal nor individualistic, neither solely personal nor cultural, neither solely internal nor external. Spirituality so understood becomes what Robert Kegan calls 'the prior ground of personality'.[12]

To restate: I define spirituality as the dynamic state of consciousness concerned with life's meaning and coherence. The essence of spirituality is found in a person's evolving ways of constructing and experiencing his or her reality, as he or she relates to and affects conceptions of the ultimate conditions of existence. These conditions, in turn, shape the character of human consciousness, the progression of human evolution, as well as a person's individual life meanings.

Essence: Redefining Holiness

Defining spirituality as a 'dynamic state of consciousness concerned with life's meaning and coherence' is particular in that it grounds the processes and drives of the spiritual within the realm of the worldly. Spirituality so defined is no longer the unseen and unexplainable force that drives a mundane and learned humanity to discover its intuitive and soulful side. Rather, as a dynamic state of consciousness, spirituality becomes ever-present in all facets of living, being informed by experience and, in turn, informing evolution. Thus, as we have already seen,

---

11. de Chardin, *The Phenomenon of Man*, 87.
12. Kegan, *The Evolving Self*, 132.

spirituality, in its dynamism, drives consciousness to find and maintain meaning and coherence as it turns its attention toward the elements of the universe individually deemed to be Ultimate. It is no secret, however, that not everyone's Ultimate is found in the realm of the Divine.

Natasha was an intelligent and charming woman who was also the CEO of a sales-oriented company. She came to see me for some supportive counseling because she was trying to cope with what she felt was a crisis in her professional life. As she toiled to move her company to the next level in its development, she found that her efforts were yielding minimal results, that her staff seemed incompetent, uncommitted, and ungrateful, that her partners exhibited bad faith, that her family was complaining about her absence, and that her stress was adversely affecting her health. She wanted to discuss her options with a non-biased listener in order to try to gain some insight into her situation, so as to make an effective decision on how best to proceed with her perceived challenges. As we sat together, session after session, I came to realize that, underneath Natasha's charming superficialities, lurked a very dark, pugnacious, utilitarian, and demeaning side.

In effect, Natasha's disposition, as it revealed itself over time, was based in a convicted, driven, and unwavering ambition toward the acquisition of money and status. All other elements of her experience (co-worker emotions and morale, family need, partner dissatisfaction, among the rest) were interpreted as deliberate attacks against her right to achieve her own personal goals. In effect, self-aggrandizement served as her Ultimate, her holy grail, her fundamental goal in living. As a result, she had slowly lost sight of the important dimensions of her life, re-casting these dimensions as annoyances and assaults on her right to devote herself completely to her self-idolization. As such, it came to light that she would often engage in reprehensible behavior such as loudly berating and humiliating her staff when they did not show her immediate and unconditional obedience, speaking scathingly of her partners when they expressed caution at a proposed course of action, defrauding her legislative and legal obligations, crudely dismissing her family's attempt at connection, and even going so far as to forget her own children on days when she had promised to pick them up. Natasha's commitment to her version of the Ultimate (self-aggrandizement) thwarted her personality, her perceptions, and her judgment, twisting her into a single-minded, distrustful, isolated, and generally hated woman. It was only by the grace of her self-protective personal narrative that she managed to shield herself from the awful truth of her situation. Recently, I learned that Natasha's company is floundering, that she has lost many key employees and supporters, and that her extended family is cutting ties with her. By devoting herself to her self-aggrandizing Ultimate, she has ironically created a solitary world in which she, and only she, can exist—the ultimate self-veneration.

Charles was introduced to me at a get-together many years ago, and we quickly became good friends. A brilliant and generous man, Charles was a judge, a philanthropist, and a patron of the arts. His fundamental conviction was that life is beautiful, that people are staggeringly entertaining, and that the world is full of wonder. To that end, although firmly an atheist in his outlook, Charles perceived a basic connection with everyone he met and every narrative he heard. He toiled tirelessly to incorporate as many people in his life as he could manage, and, as a consequence, found himself being one of the best connected men in the country. Without his social connections, he felt lonely and ostracized. In essence, connectedness was his Ultimate. Orienting himself to this Ultimate, Charles drew people to himself—the most diverse crowd I had ever encountered in a single place. He developed a pervasive reputation for compassion and understanding, and came to be known as one of the wisest proponents in his branch of the legal profession. Interestingly, although I moved away from Charles' city and can only keep in touch him through electronic means, I often encounter people who, through some sequence of coincidental connections, know of, admire, and deeply respect Charles. As such, Charles' influence has transcended even himself. As a result of this heartfelt commitment to his Ultimate (connectedness), he has inspired people to be giving, to be patient, to be compassionate, and most importantly, to see themselves in the plight of others, even at great distances. From my conversations with him, I know that Charles is unaware of his colossal influence. It can be honestly said that he is like a large boat cruising through the waters of a vast ocean. Although his eyes are fixated on the Ultimate he holds ahead of him, he leaves a wide, encompassing, and inspiring white wake behind him.

The two contrasting stories above have been presented to highlight a very real problem in the elucidation of Holiness. It is clear that our conception of the Ultimate has a seminal and profound effect on our life's course and on our construction of meaning. This, therefore, brings up a very salient question for our investigation: if we can be driven toward any end by the choice of an Ultimate, to what Ultimate should we aspire? By what standard can we compare Natasha and Charles? How are we to decide what true Holiness is?

The Pentateuchal narrative clearly and continually emphasizes the notion that true holiness cannot be achieved outside of the presence of Yahweh (Gen 26:3, 24; 28:15; 31:3; 46:4; Exodus 17:17; 19:5; 31; Leviticus 11:45; 20:26). In fact, many scholars have suggested that one of the possible themes of the Pentateuch as a whole is the theme of relationship leading to Holiness.[13] In the narrative, through the relationship Yahweh provides for His people, He guides them and leads them toward a state of greater formation and maturity. In effect, it can be argued that Yahweh gently guides the consciousness of Israel toward more attuned elements of the Divine. If spirituality is defined as a state of consciousness concerned with life's meaning and coherence, I define Holiness as the action of spirituality when spirituality focuses its efforts on the Divine. This theme of Holiness is a powerful thread that weaves through the Pentateuchal narrative, and is, to my mind, the Biblical correlate of the concept of spirituality. I believe that taken together, the concepts of spirituality and Holiness form a complementary nexus that is the very ground of the constructivist-developmental mechanism of spiritual growth. Before we can proceed to the discussion of Holiness itself, I believe that a few words on the nature of the relationship between the Divine and Human are worth covering.

In my opinion, a discussion of the relationship between the Divine and Human would do well to begin by explaining the theory of Selfhood. This theory stems from the phenomenological tradition. It impacts us all, as a universalizable and normalizing theory. It is an investigative orientation that is used in psychological, philosophical, and theological worlds, and therefore finds rooting in a very wide repertoire of scholarly exploration. In short, the phenomenological theory of Selfhood states that there are two sides to the Self: the 'I' and the 'Me'. The 'Me' component is the phenomenological factor, living in the present world, struggling to incorporate meaning, and working to maintain equilibrium. The 'Me' is the component in which the evolving constructions of consciousness reside. It is the identity that is transformed, the awareness that evolves, the conscious motivator of choice, and the seat of the personality. As an

---

13. Clines, *Theme of the Pentateuch*; Knight, *Theology as Narrative*.

element grounded in occurrence and phenomenon, 'Me' is mutable and malleable, and as such, falls under the purview of the 'I'.

The 'I' component is the meta-phenomenological factor; that is, it is the element that resides in the prior ground of phenomenon. It does not reside in the dimension of appearance, nor does it reside in the complexities of personal equilibrium. The 'I' focuses on the transcendental and conscious-driven aspects—especially those dealing with meaning and coherence. It struggles not to incorporate meaning, but rather to effect newer and more inclusively differentiated forms of meaning. Rather than working on maintaining the present equilibrium, the 'I' provides the impetus to move—to evolve—to the next level of equilibrium. The 'I' therefore is the driving force behind the growth and transformation of the 'Me'. It is the pure essence of humanity. It is evolution for the sake of evolution, constantly prompting the 'Me' to internalize another stimulus, and answer another question. The 'I' is the 'Me' transformed, the consciousness that drives awareness, the intuition that nudges action, the non-conscious motivator of growth, and the seat of spirituality. As such, 'I' carries an irreducible meaning and envisages neither multiplicity nor diversity of content, but rather unity of form, which is prior to content. In its unidirectional dynamism, 'I' focuses its attention on the realm of the Ultimate. As such, the 'I' is the fundamental driver of human growth and the very seat of Holiness. Hence, it is the responsibility of all men and women seeking Holiness to ensure that the 'I' is geared toward the Divine Ultimate.

The Self, therefore, is the combination of the 'I' and the 'Me'. As such, the Self is a complementary, self-sustaining, and forward-driven system that miraculously exists both in the here-and-now (phenomenological) and in the prior ground of the here-and-now (meta-phenomenological). Hence, Selfhood is a delicate counter-balance. Any abnegation of one aspect for the other will result in a diminished and stunted Self. Consequently, the Self is the conflagration of all that is conscious ('Me') and all that is not conscious ('I'), of all that is known and all that is unknown. The union of 'I' and 'Me', then, creates a structure that is closed but centered on the progression and transformation of consciousness—it is an ontological driver of growth. Because it contains and engenders transformations in consciousness, the confluent and congruent meeting of 'I' and 'Me' results in a powerful relationship that both challenges the moments of comfort and pacifies the moments of strife. As we shall see later, I believe that the fullest form of spiritual living lies in conscious and committed attentiveness to the confluence and congruence of the 'I' and the 'Me'. But where are the concepts of 'I' and 'Me' in the Pentateuchal narrative?

It is my contention that the relationship between Yahweh and Israel, a relationship that essentially begins in the first words of Genesis and continues beyond the denouement of Deuteronomy, is the very representation of this theory of Selfhood. In the Scriptural context, I define Self as a state of completeness, a state of congruent unity, a harmonious interrelation of all the levels of being brought to bear in a particular moment. But, true to the Pentateuchal promise of relationship, Israel cannot achieve this level of congruence—Selfhood—by its own accord or on its own terms. It is only in the company and union with the Divine that Israel can move toward this destiny. This concept of congruence is elegantly encapsulated in de Chardin's concept of Omega Point. Likening Omega to the example of Christ, de Chardin states that it is a grouping in which the personalization of the 'I' and 'Me' reach their maximum union without fusing or confounding their attributes.[14] Thus, the epitome of humankind, the zenith of our originality is not our individuality (contrary to many modern theories), but our Selfhood, as it forges unity with other Selves and with the Divine. Consequently, humanity's purpose, and in fact the very destiny of its evolution, is founded in the pursuit and protection of this unified Omega Point.

With respect to the Pentateuchal narrative, Omega Point is represented in the ever-more-unified relationship between Israel and Yahweh. To my mind, Yahweh is the epitome of 'I'—irreducible, universal, living, dynamic, and forward-pushing. He is the force that protects and guards (Leviticus 13–20) while it nurtures and encourages (Exodus 16–17). He is at the beginning of action (Exodus 7–12) and the final arbiter of growth (Exodus 32). He is, in essence, the force that helps shape and mould Israel into the Holy nation, which will influence the world (Leviticus 20:26). By corollary, Israel is the representation of 'Me'. The nation is often portrayed as struggling to understand (Numbers 14), unable to feel peace (Genesis 32), needy of reassurance (Numbers 9), deceitful and angry (Numbers 16), and even downright rebellious (Exodus 32). The further Israel distances itself from the relationship with Yahweh, the more stringent its hardships appear. Consequently, the promise of

---

14. de Chardin, *The Phenomenon of Man*, 262.

relationship is meant to alleviate this hapless floundering. Israel will become the holy nation of Yahweh, as long as it remains within Yahweh's purview. Together, Yahweh and Israel form a complementary nexus of evolution and fulfillment through which completeness arises. Similarly, together the 'I' and 'Me' form a complementary nexus of growth and understanding through which Selfhood arises. This Selfhood, driven by the power of spirituality to seek out the Divine, is what I refer to as the Pentateuchal concept of Holiness.

To my mind, the story of Holiness begins in Genesis 17. Here God says to Abraham: ". . . walk before me and be blameless." This is a pivotal moment in the narrative of the Pentateuch. Up to this point, Yahweh had a made a series of extravagant promises to Abram, but had asked for nothing in return. At this time, however, with the renewal of the original covenant as well as the renewal of Abram's very name, Yahweh places his first stipulation: the covenant will be ratified by Yahweh only if Abraham walks before Him and is blameless. In addition, this new ratified covenant is meant to be transmitted only through Abraham's family line. This is seen in the fact that Yahweh's promise is later fulfilled with the promised seed of Abraham, Isaac, and not with the surrogate son, Ishmael. Desmond Alexander outlines the strong Hebrew belief in the continuity from one generation to another.[15] It was believed that a son carried within him many of the most important traits and charges of the father. Consequently, you could recognize a family line, not only through the etymology and history of its name, but also through the consistent series of personal characteristics found among the generations. In retrospect then, the Ancestral Saga is a preparation for the founding of the covenant community, Israel. Israel is to achieve what the whole of humanity before the Flood could not understand—becoming a spiritually-driven community of true Holiness. Thus, as descendants of Abraham, the charge to blamelessness is transmitted to the entire Judeo-Christian heritage. We are charged with the notion of walking blamelessly before God.

The concept of 'walking blamelessly' is consistent with the definition of spirituality outlined in the last section. The very concept of blamelessness implies an act of consciousness and a direction to growth. After all, human beings are not born with a facile capacity to live out their lives in blamelessness. As consciousness acts upon its world, a person's capacity

---

15. Alexander, *From Paradise to the Promised Land*, 62.

to understand and grapple with issues of Holiness increases, just as differentiation, integration, and awareness increase. It is in this very grappling that humanity comes to construct its apprehensions of life's meaning, coherence, and unity. It is through this soulful struggle with Yahweh—the struggle of the grasping 'Me' with the knowing 'I' (e.g.: Genesis 32:22-31)—that the human spirit dares to push evolution forward.

A forward push, however, implies movement—a re-placement of consciousness from one order of complexity to another more intricate and inclusive one. Hence, it is no surprise that the Biblical narrative uses the metaphor of walking. Forward movement is inherent in the image of walking. It implies a deliberate and slow progression toward a particular destination. In our case, I believe that this destination is the attainment of Holiness. And the movement to get there is the action of spirituality itself.

I contend that this forward movement is the directive given to Israel by Yahweh. Through the directives and promises of the Sinai covenant, through the nurturance and care afforded Israel by Yahweh in the desert, through Yahweh, as a Pillar of Fire, physically placing Himself amidst and deliberately leading the Israelites, Yahweh fulfills His promise of guidance and directs Israel to be Holy—just as He Himself is Holy (Leviticus 11:45). Consequently, the spiritual duty of humanity is outlined. Humanity is to dedicate itself to the conscious pursuit of a relationship with the Divine. It is through this pursuit that humanity's 'Me' will find spiritual growth, evolution, and fulfillment. It is through this pursuit that humanity's 'Me' will live with meaning and coherence. As such, it is my belief that spirituality focused on the Divine—Holiness—is a Biblical exigency required of all of Abraham's descendants. And, not surprisingly, this Biblically endorsed spirituality generates the driving force behind the human progression through constructivist-developmental spiritual growth.

2. MEANING

Substance: The Meaning of Meaning

We have defined spirituality as a dynamic state of consciousness concerned with meaning and coherence. We have also invoked the message of Scripture to demonstrate that spirituality, focused on the Divine, is a godly directive and is humanity's destiny. The next logical step in the construction of our developmental framework would be to ask a simple question: what is the force, element, or stimulus that informs this spirituality? What is the impetus that causes spirituality's state of consciousness to exist and to evolve? In my opinion, this impetus is the concept of meaning.

One day, several months ago, I awoke with a sense of delight and anticipation, because I had secured this particular day as a day off from work. I felt as though I had not spent enough time with my son in the recent past, and was looking forward to passing a day with him. To that end, I telephoned his caretaker, a wonderful lady by the name of Amy, and informed her that I wanted to keep my son with me for the day. Her response was cordial and agreeable. Thereafter, my little boy and I had a fun-filled day of excursions, movies and junk food, arriving home in the early evening, exhausted and ready for the bedtime ritual. About an hour later, I found myself sitting on the couch alone, smiling, satisfied, and content to have been able to spend a day with this little boy who brings me so much joy.

And that is when the telephone call arrived. The call was from one of my closest friends whose children were also being taken care of by Amy. She kindly and gently informed me that Amy was very upset all day and that, although she may have sounded agreeable to my decision to keep my son at home for the day, she had actually been riddled with deep concerns and doubts about my reasons. In her estimation, it was a distinct possibility that she had offended me in some way and that I was wavering in my trust of her caretaking abilities. She had recalled several instances over the past several months where she felt uncertain and insecure about her own abilities, and these doubts culminated on this very day with the appearance of my decision. As such, she ended the day in tears and felt too embarrassed to speak to me directly, as she did not want to show her vulnerability so explicitly. I was bewildered, to say the least. What to me was an innocent and responsible action was, to her, a serious infraction on her sense of competence and autonomy. What to me was a simple act of transferring factual information about my son's whereabouts was, to her, information of my supposed displeasure with her, both personally and professionally. As a result of the collision of these two worlds, Amy and I now had an interpersonal situation that required resolution and correction—an undertaking that would most certainly require a significant amount of energy on both our parts.

This story is illustrative of a very common situation in human discourse—the clashing of two world views, where each view interprets the bare events and stimuli of a situation in its own unique, and inimitable way. This process of interpretation is what is commonly referred to as meaning-making, and the substrate of this process is meaning itself.

I define meaning as constructed information that informs spirituality. As such, the process of meaning-making is foundational to the formation and development of the constructivist-developmental framework of spiritual growth.

In trying to grasp the concept of meaning, I direct my attention to the spiritual space between the occurrence of a stimulus and a person's response to it. This is the arena of Spirit in which a stimulus is internally apprehended, interpreted, and made sense of—the place where it actually becomes, or fails to become, a salient event for that person. So important is this concept, that practically every personality psychology and insightful theology that influences counselors, care-givers, and Spiritual Leaders directs itself in some way to the "zone of mediation where meaning is made."[16] How we grasp what we apprehend will be settled in this zone of mediation, where a person interprets his or her world and makes personal sense of stimuli.

Kegan uses the word 'meaning' to refer simultaneously to an epistemological and ontological activity.[17] According to him, meaning is about knowing *and* being; it is about theory making on the one hand (spirituality), and investment and commitment to the Self, on the other (evolution of spirituality). Thus, information presented to the consciousness is filtered, taken up and assimilated (construction). It is interpreted through the filter of present spirituality (meaning-making). Finally, it informs the consciousness and promotes the attenuation of coherence and unity. As we shall see, both constructivism and developmentalism insist on a recognition that behind the form of objects, there exists "a personal process which creates it".[18] In agreement with Kegan, I believe

---

16. Kegan, *Evolving Self*, 2. I have liberally paraphrased Kegan in the presentation of this definition.
17. Kegan, *The Evolving Self*, 8.
18. Kegan, *The Evolving Self*, 13.

it is through this creative activity of constructing information that each person proves himself or herself to be a meaning-making organism.

William Perry, writing in the 1970s, believed that meaning-making is an essentially ontological characteristic of humanity. In other words, our very nature is to make meaning; meaning-making is one of the defining and fundamental markers of what it means to be human.[19] As such, we conclude from this that there cannot be an experience, an apprehension of a stimulus, or a relational action of any kind that is somehow separate from, or independent of the inexorable processes of personal meaning-making. We *create* the sense we perceive in our lives. As Kegan says, "Human being is the composing of meaning."[20] This notion that we constitute our very apprehensions through meaning-making cuts across the domains of philosophy, psychology, and theology. In the words of Viktor Frankl: "[Humanity's] search for meaning is the primary drive in [its] life and not a secondary rationalization of instinctual drives. This meaning is specific and unique in that it can be fulfilled by [human beings] alone."[21] It is my firm belief that humanity's essence is contained in the movement and evolution of meaning-making.

The story of meaning-making starts at infancy and progresses throughout the entire lifecycle, gaining levels of abstraction and sophistication as it progresses. As such, the development of meaning-making takes us out of the infant's world of pure subjectivity and places us squarely in the adult world, which is explicitly mediated by meaning. The world of the infant is no bigger than the proverbial nursery. It is a world of physiology, instinct, impression, and reaction. Bernard Lonergan states that it is a world of immediate experience, of the given as given, of image and affect without the distractions of concept, judgment, deliberation, or choice. Therefore, it is a world of pleasure and pain, hunger and thirst, food and drink, rage, satisfaction, and sleep. As consciousness develops, however, one's world expands exponentially. Symbols, such as language, come to represent not only what is present, but also what is absent, what is past, and what is future.[22] In fact, theorists such as Charles Pierce and John Seobock believe that all human communication is fundamentally semiological—a semiology that develops from sensorimotor to formal

---

19. Perry, *Development in the College Years*, 32.
20. Kegan, *The Evolving Self*, 11.
21. Frankl, *Man's Search for Meaning*, 32.
22. Lonergan, *Method in Theology*, 78.

operational capabilities.²³ In the formal operational mode, symbols are manipulated to reflect not only the factual, but also the possible, the theoretical, the ideal, and the normative.²⁴ In other words, these communications express not only what we have found to be of personal import, but also all we care to learn from the memories of our neighbors, from the common sense of the community, from the pages of literature, from the labors of our teachers, from the investigations of scientists, from the experience of saints, and from the mediations of philosophers and theologians. In light of this, it becomes clear that meaning-making is inexorably intertwined with the selective, interpretive, and executive capacities that many psychologists have associated with Selfhood, and in fact, stands at their roots.²⁵ Therefore, this conception of meaning-making is an organizing principle which is the prior ground of spirituality, and therefore is also the prior ground of the resultant thoughts, affects, and relations.

In speaking of the prior relationship of meaning to life activities, Lonergan states that the essence of meaning is held in the context of questioning and is determined not only by experience but also by personal understanding and judgment.²⁶ The full act of meaning-making, then, is also an act of judging. This judgment is invoked in the settling of the status of an object of thought—whether an object is merely an object of thought, a mathematical entity, an actual thing lying in the world of human experience, or a transcendent reality beyond the perception of the empirical. As such, active meanings come with judgments of value, decisions, and actions. Lonergan states that it is this addition of the layer of judgment that makes possible a world mediated by meaning. It is this judgment, which gives meaning its structure and unity, which arranges it in an orderly whole partly known and familiar, partly surrounded in shadow.²⁷ It is meaning that mediates our construction of the 'real world'

---

23. Peirce, *Collected Papers*, and Seobock, *Signs*; Piaget, *Constructions of Reality*.

24. Lonergan, *Method in Theology*, 80; Boden, *Piaget*, 63; Seobock, *Signs*; Piaget, *Constructions of Reality*.

25. For more, please see Kegan, *The Evolving Self*, 29; Boden. *Piaget*, 46; Kohlberg, *Moral Stages* ,72; Lonergan, *Method in Theology*; Lonergan, *Insight*;, Perry, *College Years*, ch. 1.

26. Lonergan, *Method in Theology*, 74.

27. Lonergan, *Method in Theology*, 81.

as well as our construction of the 'Me'. As such, meaning-making is the very seat of the 'Self'.

Essence: The Prior Ground of Story

We have discussed what meaning is, but how does meaning work? Can we find a basis for this concept in the Biblical account? I believe that the Pentateuchal narrative gives us a unique insight into the mechanism by which meaning functions. As we mentioned above, meaning is constructed information that informs spirituality. In the Biblical account, the definition is slightly different: meaning is constructed information that informs Holiness. Regardless of the sphere in which we apply the definition, meaning is the prior ground of spirituality, and therefore thought, affect, and relation. It is the stimulus and the impetus through which attitudes and behaviors are mediated. The Pentateuchal narrative models this type of prior-ground relationship, as it progresses through its delivery of story.

From the early chapters of Genesis, Yahweh generously provides a series of powerful promises to the Patriarchs. In fact, the entire Primeval cycle can be summarized as a slow descent of human consciousness into a self-focused, self-aggrandizing, and fragmented state, degenerating slowly from the utopia of Eden to the segregation and alienation of Babel.[28] Therefore, the Patriarchal promises, coming on the heels of this descent, are representative of a dramatic turn in Israel's history—a turn founded in the grace of Yahweh, and mediated through a single family line. It is generally agreed by scholars that one of the promises made to Abraham and his descendants was the promise of seed (or descendants). Since the purpose of this section is not to explore the ramifications of the actual promise but to illustrate the mechanics through which meaning functions, I will not further discuss the intricacies of the promise *per se*. But I will state a fundamental aspect of the Pentateuchal narrative that illustrates the point of this section very well: as of the moment the Divine promise appears in the narrative flow, the entire thrust of the plot thereafter is embedded in the matrix of the fulfillment of the promise. That is, although there are many ways to view individual episodes that arise throughout the Pentateuchal storyline, when looked at from the teleoscopic view of the entire progression of the narrative, the episodes

---

28. Moberly, *The Old Testament*, 58.

all fall within the purview of the Divine promise. Every action, reaction, directive, challenge, triumph, fear, and ambition is interpreted against the background of promise. Consequently, just as meaning acts as the prior ground of information to the movement of spirituality, so the Divine promise acts as the prior ground to the movement of the story itself—it is the information that informs the pursuit of Holiness. I will set forth an illustration of this point.

The beauty and inspiration of Biblical art can be seen in its ability to teach both in its specific incarnations and in its more far-reaching narrative manifestations. As such, the story of Abraham sacrificing Isaac at Yahweh's command is a powerful lesson of unconditional obedience of the Great 'I'. It is also a story of redemption as both Abraham and Isaac are saved from the terrifying consequences of the potential sacrifice (Genesis 22). In contrast to this episode which presented terrifying possibilities, the story of the Manna and quails provided to the people of Israel while in the desert demonstrates Yahweh's deep concern, compassion, and nurturance for the struggling 'Me'. It is a narrative fostering trust and faith in the Divine, which often lies unseen and subtle (Exodus 16). These beautiful stories taken separately and specifically, teach humanity about the saving power of God's grace—both through redemption and nurturance. Taken more teleoscopically, however, a different pattern arises—a pattern informed by the promise of seed.

In the Abraham and Isaac episode, Abraham is asked to willingly sacrifice his son, his descendant, his seed. Not only was this son divinely promised and very difficult to come by (Genesis 21:1-8), he was also the only progeny afforded to Abraham by his legitimate wife. As such, the directive to sacrifice the boy was tantamount to a deliberate eradication of the progress of Yahweh's promise, and therefore of the covenant that bound Abraham to Yahweh. Therefore, Abraham's act of obedience is suddenly held up to this stark information—and thereby rendered in a new and qualitatively different light. No longer is this episode solely about his action as those of an obedient man, unquestioningly following the will of his God. Rather, the story's message now transforms into the highlighting of Yahweh Himself as not only the giver of the promise, but also its defender and its protector. The promise is elucidated as the gift of Yahweh to Abraham and not as Abraham's entitlement from Yahweh. Through this episode, the relationship between Yahweh, Abraham, and the promise is clarified. The theme of the Divine promise of seed has qualitatively redefined and selectively highlighted certain aspects of the narrative—aspects that would be understood differently were the meaningful filter of the promise not present.

Similarly, in the story of the Manna and quails, we come face-to-face with a generous and giving God. But is that the crux of the story? Yet again, the meaning constitutive function of the Divine promise of seed makes its influence visible. Backlit by the presence of this promise, the sending of the Manna and quails into the desert qualitatively transforms it into an action that transcends simple generosity. It is the act of God, who has promised a long and fruitful line of descendants, actively taking a role in the preservation of that line in times of scarcity. No longer is humanity to look out for itself, no longer does Israel have to bear the responsibility for proliferation alone. Yahweh Himself, the Great 'I', joins in the action and by so doing, proves Himself to be faithful to the health of Israel—the worldly 'Me'—but also to His promise of seed which transcends the ages.

The transcendent and transformative function provided in the narrative by the Pentateuchal Divine promises is a powerful model for the function of meaning in our lives. Just as the Divine promise was always present (whether subtly or candidly) and affected the outcomes and actions of the various players in the narrative, so meaning is always present, in subtle or dramatic manners, in the matrix of everyday life. Just as the presence of the Divine promise qualitatively transformed the depth, drive, and significance of the Pentateuchal episodes, so meaning, as the prior ground of thought, affect, and relation, qualitatively transforms the content and shape of these elements. Just as loyalty to the Divine promise is translated as Holiness in the Biblical narrative, so meaning, as the prior ground of thought, affect, and relation, informs that state of consciousness that is spirituality. In the end, meaning and spirituality, much in the same manner as Science and Faith, are two faces and phases of the same process—the process of constructing a state of consciousness that coheres. Hence, meaning-making is the fundamental driving force behind the Divinely endorsed condition of spirituality, and is thus a critical component of spiritual growth.

3. EVOLUTION

Substance: Progressing Through Evolution

We have come to an understanding of the process of spirituality, and we have highlighted meaning-making as the activity which informs spirituality and thereby promotes human evolution. In this section of defining terms, we are left with one final concept to clarify: the concept of evolution. I have often mentioned this word and have named it as the end-result of the synergy between meaning and spirituality. I will now turn my attention to a specific defining of this very important concept. It is my belief that, armed with a clear conception of spirituality, meaning, and evolution, our discussion of the constructivist-developmental stages of spiritual growth will proceed with greater ease and completeness.

When Andre came to me for counseling, he was interested in tackling his feelings of general loneliness. For years, he had been unable to shake the sense of personal isolation that was instilled in him by a dismissive, disconnected, and self-serving familial home. Chief among the relationships that caused him distress was the one with his sister, Joanne. Throughout their entire lives, Joanne was deeply concerned with her own success, often overlooking Andre's hurt feelings and fundamental need for companionship. So segregated was Joanne from Andre's world that, in her youth, she would often go out of her to opine on her general disrespect for his academic and professional choices, her displeasure at his choice of friends, and even her derision at his fashion sense. As the years passed, however, Joanne began to soften, to understand how life's complexities are not so black-and-white, and to better appreciate her brother's stances on many relational issues. Having gotten married herself, she came into a more comprehensive understanding of the interdependent complexities of married life and the vital importance of trusted friendships. As such, she began reaching out to Andre.

In one of his later sessions, Andre came into my office, bewildered and touched. He had just come through a difficult time, having been laid-off and under tremendous financial stress. During these stressful times, his habitual sense of loneliness and inadequacy gained ascendency over his better judgment, and dark clouds seemed to fill his world. In addition, he did not have the resources to engage in activities that normally brought him comfort, such as a nice dinner out, a few hours at the art gallery, or an evening of live theater. During this particular session, Andre relayed to me that his bemusement stemmed from a remarkably loving and generous gift from none other than his sister Joanne. Having perceived his stress and anxiety, Joanne had decided to help Andre by sending him a gift certificate to a prominent local restaurant, as well as two tickets to see the latest theatrical sensation at one of the city's premiere theaters. Her card to him was simple and touching: "You've been stressed. You deserve this. Have fun and be happy." Even days later, Andre was speechless.

Joanne's story demonstrates spiritual progression. As time passed, she moved from a state of youthful self-centeredness to one of connected caring, from a stance of judgment to one of love, and from a position of challenge to one of deep compassion. Joanne's being had unfolded its possibilities and found new, more integrated ways of orienting itself to Andre and, in fact, the entire world. She had truly moved beyond the person she had been and had now found the courage to show her true, connected, and generous spirit. It is just such a story of progression that is illustrative of the concept of evolution.

For the purposes of the growth framework presented in this book, I define human evolution as an integrated and progressing sense of responsible connectedness. A hefty sum of words, to be sure . . . . But each word is carefully chosen to complement the meaning of the term and to bring about a full formulation of what evolution signifies in the constructivist-developmental framework. With the reader's indulgence, I will parse the various pieces of this comprehensive definition.

I have begun the definition with the concept of integration. What does this term encompass for our investigation and why is it first? To my mind, the concept of integration is much more than simply a concept on inclusion. Inclusion implies membership, validation, and relevance within a particular event, concept, or scheme. It is a function of being received, of being thought of, and of being taken into account. It implies a certain degree of presence on the part of that which is 'included', even though the importance or relevance of that presence is not alluded to by the term. Hence, it is an element of belonging, of participation, and often, of empowerment to that which is included.

As an illustration, I am reminded of the events that often take place during a democratic election. In an election, leadership hopefuls outline their plans for the next several years, and proceed, over the next several months, to drum up support for their proposed solutions on many of the most prominent issues of the day. In the formulations of their platforms, leadership hopefuls will typically attempt to take many high profile issues into account, and propose a socially acceptable, and expediently applicable solution to each issue, in order to win over converts in the electoral pool. The winner is often the candidate who can win over the greatest number of electors, based on the appeal of each of the elements of his or her platform. Candidates propound the advantages of a restrictive corporate policy in an otherwise cynical and overworked population, of prohibiting abortion because it violates a fundamental reverence for life, of funding post-secondary education to help young voters achieve greater levels of career success, and of cutting general taxes to alleviate the strain being placed on the wallets of overtaxed electors. As a leadership hopeful progresses throughout a campaign, he or she makes a concerted effort to take into account—to include—the needs and wants of the most powerful sectors of the voting society. As such, the electors in these sectors feel empowered, validated, seen, and important. So powerful is this need of inclusion that often the candidate most able to convince the greater number of people of inclusion, will walk away with the victory.

My conception of 'integration', however, is much greater and farther reaching than the concept of inclusion. Although it encompasses the aspects of inclusion stated above, it makes its influence felt much more powerfully in the mechanics of events and persons. To my mind, integration is the very hard work involved in a *congruent* act of inclusion. In this act, the various and extant elements of the *entire* situation, (as understood by the integrator) intertwine and interrelate to produce a harmonious and elegant solution, in which all the various complexities of the parts find inclusion. This solution, often a combination of the physical, emotional, spiritual, and transcendent, is greater than the solutions of simple inclusion because it gears itself specifically to the health and progression of the *whole*, and not merely to a single aspect of the system. Since all systemic, personal, and transcendental elements have a voice in the process of integration, I call it a congruent process. Since all elements at hand are intertwined in a cohesive harmony, I call the object of integration a complete solution. And since, through these two processes, integration impacts on a person's mode of making meaning, it is a foundational force in the progression of any mechanism that is spiritual.

As such, inclusion is about acting, whereas integration is about being. Inclusion often results in quick gratification, whereas integration takes time to study the ramifications of solutions, and therefore delays gratification. Inclusion is about attitude, whereas integration is about spiritual identity. Inclusion is a compartmentalized activity, whereas integration is a personal and congruent presence in the 'whole'.

Returning therefore to our leadership hopefuls, we find that a single candidate is conducting her campaign through the propagation of integrated solutions, rather than simple inclusive solutions. She is the candidate that considers whether or not the reasonable reactions expected from her corporate policies would drive unemployment rates to a level in which abortion is more likely. She is the candidate that considers whether her anti-abortion stance is truly in harmony with her taxation obligations of policing her anti-abortion law and funding appropriate and healthy alternatives for the vast sector of the populous that cannot afford an alternative. She is the candidate that balances the effect of her desire to give financial bonuses to young families with the effect of her desire to fund post-secondary education, thereby essentially encouraging later stage marriage and family formation. Therefore, the candidate's mind is on the creation of a complete leadership package that addresses the whole of societal functioning—physical, emotional, relational, and spiritual—in each of her decisions. It is not merely an accumulated collection of intelligent, yet compartmentalized, answers to perfunctory questions. This candidate works to attend to the whole situation, rather than simply paying attention to the various elements of the whole.

As the first element in our definition of evolution, integration stipulates that a personal alignment to the whole is a fundamental prerequisite to the development of consciousness. In other words, I believe that it is not possible to evolve without first weathering an experience of integration. Inclusion may promote the development of thought, of affect, of relationship, and even of spiritual elements, but it is only integration that opens the door to a foundational and qualitative shift in the ground of perception—the consciousness—that results in permanent change (evolution). It is for this reason that integration is the first term in my definition of human evolution.

The next term I use to define evolution is progress. In this context, I do not refer to 'progress' as meaning the forward thrust of invention that is the legacy of scientific investigation. Rather, I am referring to a process of personal development. Webster's dictionary defines development as the process of 'making active, to move from an original position to one of greater opportunity for effective use, to grow and differentiate along natural lines, to grow through a process of natural growth as set out by evolution or successive changes.'[29] Hence, my use of the term 'progress' in the definition of evolution is meant to highlight the paramount role of successive changes within the consciousness of the evolving person. In addition, these successive changes move from an original position to one of greater complexity, greater viability (with respect to the environment), and greater levels of integration. In our illustrative story, Joanne had fundamentally progressed in her growth, changing into a very different person from the one she had been in youth—a person who could now apprehend the totality of a relational situation and act appropriately so as to achieve further connection. In essence, therefore, this term in the definition of evolution is pointing toward a movement of consciousness from one stage and level to another, rather than a refining of the current construction of epistemology. It is a directional, yet process-oriented movement that reacts to meaning-making and attempts to alter consciousness to resolve apparent conflicts and contradictions. As such, it is the natural follow-through of integration and the precursor of qualitative transformation. But where does this process occur?

This question is answered by the third term in our definition—'sense'. A 'sense' is usually associated with something felt, something gleaned, something known even if this 'something' is not understood, perceived, or purposeful. As such, I use the word 'sense' to indicate those elements of personal knowledge that we come to know through super-rational means. That is, a 'sense', by my understanding, is an awareness that comes into being through the actions of the more subtle levels of being, the levels that are the prior the ground of thought, feeling, and relation. Thus, this term in the definition of evolution appeals to consciousness. It is not thought, affect, or relationship that must progress, but rather, it is the fundamental ground of those elements, which is consciousness—the super-rational sense that must progress through integration in order for evolution to occur. As such, harkening back to the story of Joanne and Andre, it is not that Joanne's mind had changed over time. It was rather

---

29. Merriam-Webster On-Line, Merriam-Webster Incorporated, www.m-w.com, accessed on November 12, 2006.

that her underlying consciousness, her fundamental sense of how the world worked, had shifted.

As of this point, we have constructed our definition to a significant extent. Evolution is an integrated and progressing sense. Two more terms are left for our elucidation.

The first of these terms is the concept of responsibility. Entire volumes could be written on this vast and universal concept. Our treatment of it in this section, however, will focus on a specific aspect of the term: responsibility to the Self. Having already defined 'Selfhood' as the congruent interrelation of 'I' and 'Me', I am now moving to an important activity of Selfhood—the maintenance and nurturance of the Self. Maintaining the Self, then, is an active undertaking, involving nothing less than a total engagement of the consciousness in the propagation and sustenance of the hard-won Self. As such, this term is important in our definition of evolution because it implies that one of the pillars of integrated progress is an attentiveness to the sustenance and nurturance of the Self. Therefore, this type of responsibility demands that each person attend to the phenomenological aspects of life ('Me') as well as to the meta-phenomenological aspects of being ('I'). It is a natural correlate of the balanced preservation of Self in a culture that tends to promote denial and abnegation of Self. It is the attenuation of autonomy (discussed at greater length later) and the attentiveness afforded the preferences of that autonomy. It is the fostering of the Self we discover, the maintaining of the Self we become, and the surrendering of the Self we share. We cannot relate to other Selves except through the action and filter of our own Selves. The term 'responsible' in our definition of evolution, then, is the term meant to address the issue of the importance of the progressing sense—the very consciousness—within an evolving person. As we well know, however, persons do not exist in a vacuum. We involve ourselves in our surroundings, in our neighbors and in our events. As such, the final term in our definition of evolution is 'connectedness'.

The entire process of integration, of progression, and of responsible consciousness is of no use if it does not support further interconnection of the evolving person with his or her world. Hence, the term connectedness is not meant to indicate a connection with a particular person, place or thing. Rather, I believe that connectedness in this context is meant to indicate a consciousness that perceives the unity, the coherence, and the interrelation of all elements contained within an individual life. It is the foundation of relatedness, reciprocity, and personal surrender—three elements that are paramount to the constructive practice of a life dedicated to Holiness. As I shall highlight later, it is the other side of the responsibility coin as it progresses through integration and transformation. It is the element responsible for empathy, love, insight, awareness, inner peace, and humility. It is the progressing and ever-more comprehensive sense (consciousness) of interrelation that is the final hallmark of a developing Self. As such, it is not enough to look for the maintenance and sustenance of one's Self (responsibility). It is rather a question of sustaining and maintaining one's Self in a progressing and ever-more complex system of interrelations in which reciprocity and surrender reign.

Evolution is the integrated and progressing sense of responsible connectedness. As such, it takes all levels of being into account. It works its acts of development on the consciousness of humanity, rather than on its behavior, knowledge, or activities alone. It is the movement of the prior ground of Self—consciousness. Therefore, evolution is a fundamentally spiritual concept, undergirding the state of consciousness that is spirituality. Evolution is the progressing *movement* of spirituality from one state of consciousness to another greater state. In other words, evolution is the movement of spirituality itself as it comes to 're-cognize', 're-know', and re-organize its construction of consciousness, in order to be more integrated, more responsible, and more connected with all the elements of the world in which it must function.[30] As we progress through our constructivist-developmental conception of spiritual growth, the notion of evolution will hold as central a place as the concepts of spirituality and meaning.

Essence: Progressing Through Genesis

Having defined 'evolution' for our context, I now turn my attention to grounding the concept of evolution in the Pentateuchal narrative. Although many individual examples abound throughout the story, I have decided to take a longer-range view of the narrative. My goal is not so much to redefine evolution as it can be found in the Pentateuch. Rather, my goal is to explore how a significant and foundational portion of the Pentateuchal narrative indicates not only human evolution, but also the

---

30. Kegan, *Evolving Self*, 265.

direction that evolution is meant to take. The main text relevant to our discussion here will be the Primeval Cycle found in Genesis 1–11.

Starting from the first few words of the Creation account, the Biblical narrative makes several things very clear: the universe is created by God, it is created deliberately, and everything was placed as it was according to a Divine design. Thus, the notion of order is very prominent in the Creation account. There is a strong emphasis on the harmony of Creation, as well as on the harmony that lives on after the Creative act. I agree with the assessment of Thomas Mann, who believes that the themes set out in the first chapters of Genesis, are the very ones that infuse the rest of the Pentateuchal narrative.[31] Through the Primeval examples of Creation and the placement of Humanity upon Creation, the Pentateuch is preoccupied with a world in which order derives from a dedication of consciousness to all things Divine.

The crowning moment of Creation, according to the Pentateuchal narrative, is the Creation of Humanity. Not only does God create the perfect environment within which humanity can thrive, He also creates and blesses humanity, directs it to multiply, and charges it with the caretaking of Creation (Genesis 1–2). In effect, humanity is crowned as God's vice-regent on Earth, uniquely reflecting something of God's nature and sovereignty within the scheme of Creation (humanity was after all created in God's image). This nature and sovereignty is furthered by the conversational and ubiquitous relationship humanity enjoys with its Creator. Thus, humanity is charged with two serious and Divine directives: the responsibility to maintain completeness and unity with God, and the responsibility to watch over His Creation. In the charge of responsibility, however, God stipulates a single provision that is forbidden: Adam and Eve shall not eat of the fruit of a particular Tree. To my mind, this is a fundamental twist in the story of creative responsibility. The notion of human responsibility carries with it a delicate counter-balance: humanity must strive to live up to the great task of safeguarding Creation, but, it must also ensure that it not overstep its boundaries with respect to its essence as a creation of God. In the narrative, this harmony is stressed as the first link in God's relational chain. The proper relationship between God and humanity is properly understood as the relation between the one who commands and guides ('I'), and the one who is moulded and led ('Me'). As such, humanity's responsibility, in spite of

31. Mann, *The Book of Torah*, 14.

the presence of free will, demands that it sees itself as not too great, nor too little in the scheme of Creation. This human responsibility, in my opinion, is one of the founding principles of humanity's destiny as the Holy people of God.

I begin with this story because I believe it carries within it some powerful lessons for our concept of evolution. First among these lessons is the notion that God created the universe so as to perfectly meet our needs. Many skeptics have decried this doctrine, questioning how humanity's needs could possibly be met in the culture of this challenging and often contravening world. I believe that the resolution to this question lies not in a menial justification of the beauty of God's work (a traditional and trite response to a complex and entitled question). Rather, I believe the resolution to this question lies in the transformation of the consciousness of the questioner. To what is the Creation narrative referring when it indicates that God's Creation is perfect for humanity? My answer is at once simple and disturbing.

I believe that in relating the events of Creation, the Pentateuchal narrative is telling us deep truths about our *spiritual* well-being and our quest for Holiness. Therefore, the Creation of the world is exactly as it should be in order to promote our spiritual evolution toward a unity with Yahweh. It is not that Creation is flawed because life is challenging. Rather, it is that Creation is *perfect* because life is challenging—it is challenging in the exact ways relevant to and encouraging of the evolution of humanity. We are not entitled to a state of earthly bliss. Much like the infant who only learns to walk by overcoming the resistance introduced by the floor on his straining leg muscles, so humanity can grow and develop only by exerting itself in the integration of the challenges (the resistance) introduced into its life by the nature of Creation. For this reason, I state that my view is disturbing. I do not believe that there are Biblical promises that indicate Yahweh's intention to spoil humanity into complacency. I do not believe a perfect Creation is that in which all wants are met, leaving us devoid of any and all impetus to evolve and integrate the new. Rather, I believe that the challenges and responsibilities presented by Creation as it is, are the very challenges and responsibilities required for the progression of spirituality and Holiness. Thus, since God's Creation is perfect, the challenges faced by Adam and Eve are also perfect. It is, in fact, the veiled story of this book to outline a conception of how humanity weathers God's perfect challenges.

In summary then, the opening of the Primeval cycle, by outlining the circumstances and conditions of a perfect and orderly Creation, stipulates for humanity the state and relationship to which it must aspire throughout its exercise of free will. But, fundamental to the task of humanity is a unified relationship with God and a delicately balanced sense of responsibility. In developing the opening of the story, it is my belief that the remainder of the Primeval cycle outlines the story of the breakdown of this perfect and orderly state of affairs. Through its narration of the breakdown (from the expulsion from the Garden of Eden to its climax in the fragmentation of the Tower of Babel), the Pentateuchal narrative indicates what it believes is necessary for the progression of human evolution.

Our story of evolutionary descent begins in the Garden of Eden, with the purposeful disobedience of God by Adam and Eve. The consequences of this act involved an alienation of humanity from the ground, an expulsion from the Garden, a promise of further hardships, and a prohibition to ever return through the now-guarded Gate (Genesis 3:24). This episode denotes the first instance of breach within the Divine-Human relationship—the consequence of humanity's deliberate act of overstepping the bounds of the Divinely ordained relationship, and acting irresponsibly. Throughout the narrative of the Primeval cycle, the theme of humanity trying to take godly initiative will repeatedly be highlighted, along with its dire and pain-producing effects. From Adam and Eve eating the apple (Genesis 3:6), to Abel's murder (Genesis 4:8), to Lamech's boastful arrogance (Genesis 4:23), through the Flood (Genesis 6), and into the decision to build the Tower of Babel (Genesis 11), the irresponsible drive of humanity, increasingly disconnected from Yahweh, acting on its own accord and giving in to the illusion of self-sufficiency, continuously creates adversity, as the human consciousness sinks evermore into a state of lonely ignorance. This is reminiscent of what was stated earlier regarding the relationship between the 'I' and the 'Me': as long as the 'Me' acts alone, it is doomed to circle in its present state of knowing, floundering to create sense of the new impetus, in a world no longer integrated enough to accept the complexities of this impetus. It is only in union with the 'I' that the 'Me' can achieve transformational growth and adapt to new and more integrated ways of being. It is only through a deference to Yahweh that humanity can be transformed into the Holy nation of God. Thus, the progression throughout the Primeval cycle, the progression of the ever-more glorified 'Me', illustrates a rapid degradation of the integration of awareness in the human consciousness. The people who walk away from the Tower are very different from the ones who are expelled from the Garden. The descent has reached a new and more comprehensive level of chaos, irresponsibility, immediate gratification, and pursuit of personal wants.

In addition to the importance of the relationship between God and humanity ('I' and 'Me'), these episodes relate the importance of integrated knowledge. Yahweh's directives always address the needs of the current situation as well as the potential complexities of future ramifications. Although Cain is expelled, he is marked in order to prevent retaliation against him (4:15); although Yahweh destroys life on Earth with the Flood, he retains a remnant through which to rebuild the majesty of Creation (Genesis 9); although Adam and Eve effectively lose both their sons to a single tragic event, Yahweh ensures that they receive a third son, thereby protecting their family line (Genesis 4:25). As such, the integrated wisdom of Yahweh was generously available to humanity as it pursued its conversant and daily relationship with Him (in the Garden). A return to a state of union with Yahweh, a reunification of the 'I' with the 'Me', would therefore require a re-integration of the knowledge that was lost during the centuries of descent. If the story of the redemption of Israel is the story of the struggle to return to a state of union with Yahweh (the Tabernacle often being interpreted as a paradigm of the Garden of Eden)[32], then the first lesson to be learned is that of the importance of integration. Acting on its own terms, humanity lost sight of many elements intrinsic to harmony and relationship. Acting in accordance with Yahweh, Israel starts on the road to regain that level of considered integration in its dealings and its adventures. Hence, a powerful lesson of the descent into chaos is that of the importance and primacy of Divine union, which results in the achievement of greater knowledge integration among the people of Israel.

But of course, the story does not end at integration. The extent of humanity's descent into the chaos of self-sufficiency implies that the road back to spiritual health is not an instantaneous process. Rather, a return to the state of unity prescribed by the conditions of perfect Creation requires that several steps of reconciliation take place. As such, the movement from the Tower of Babel to the unity of the Tabernacle

---

32. For more on this, please see Mann, *The Book of Torah*.

involved many episodes and many tribulations. It was in fact a slow and laborious process, taken on by both Yahweh ('I') and the people of Israel ('Me'). It is clear from the one-sided response of the Primeval cycle that humanity's participation in the relational unity with Yahweh is paramount to the success of the relationship. As such, the process back to spiritual health is not simply a process of Divine decree: it is also a process of human participative progression. Therefore, it took a lengthy and convoluted process to breakdown the conditions of Creation, and it would take an equal pursuit of progress to reverse the effects of those dismal years.

In summary then, I have stated that the descent into chaos must be reversed if the perfect and orderly conditions set out at Creation are going to be re-created. In order for this process to come to fruition, however, several aspects of the descent of consciousness must be reversed—namely, a reclaiming of proper responsibility by humanity, a unified relationship with Yahweh, an ability to act in an integrative manner, and an understanding of the progressive stages necessary to reverse the effects of the Fall. I believe that there is one more element that requires closer attention: the element of connectedness.

I have often wondered why the story of the Tower of Babel came after the story of the Great Flood in the account of the descent of human consciousness. Surely, a cataclysmic event like the Flood is the very bottom of the *de*-volution barrel; surely the death of humanity is the greatest price that can be paid for the abdication of the Divinely decreed responsibility. According to the Pentateuchal narrative, however, the final episode in the descent of humanity before the new beginning ushered in by Abraham is the fragmentation of humanity at the Tower of Babel. As a result of its position in the narrative flow, this story highlights the climax of the de-volution of human consciousness. The Tower story is the account of how humanity took it upon itself to build a massive structure in order to make a great name for itself. In other words, it was an act of self-aggrandizement, of the glorification of the human consciousness—the 'Me'—for its own sake. It was the clearest and most flagrant form of self-worship described by the narrative of the Primeval cycle. Therefore, to my mind, it is not so much the act of building a Tower to reach the heavens that was intrinsically destructive. Rather, it was the virtual deification of the human consciousness which finally brought about the last fall in a series of falls.

The consequence of these actions was the complete fragmentation of humanity. Whereas the Flood destroyed life on Earth, the remnant in the Ark was a family line. Hence, the Flood had taken humanity and life off the face of the Earth, but it had not been meant to take away human collaboration and connection. When normal life patterns had been re-established after the Flood, however, the progress of the descent of human consciousness literally picked up where it left off. Stories of debauchery, drunkenness, and lust were all ultimately crowned by the story of arrogance and self-deification: the story of the Tower. As a result of Yahweh's response, humanity walks away from the Tower alone, segregated, unheard, unable to communicate, unable to see, and unable to stand together. As such, the progression of de-volution takes us from a simple act of disobedience in a perfect Garden to a grand act of self-glorification and denial at the base of the Tower. The final result—a result worse than death as far as the Pentateuchal narrative is concerned: aloneness, disconnection, disengagement, isolation, irresponsibility, and narrowness, all within a context where there no longer is the possibility of forging a relationship with Yahweh. Hence, the lesson is clear: connection is a Divine and powerful gift to humanity. It is a fundamental element of human spiritual health and, as illustrated by the story of the Tower, is a primary goal to be pursued. Healthy human progress ends in a retrieval of this primal sense of connection.

A summation of the themes highlighted in this section correlate directly to my definition of evolution stated earlier. The Pentateuchal narrative states that Creation was an act of perfection. Therefore, the destiny of humanity is to re-create the consciousness and conditions involved in that perfect sphere of relation with the Divine. The descent of human consciousness into chaos, however, outlines the loss of the most important elements of consciousness: relationship, responsibility, integration, and connection. The return to this utopian state is not a miraculous one-step solution. Rather, it is a slow and deliberate progression through the perfect challenges presented to us by God's perfect Creation. As such, I contend that the Pentateuchal narrative, taken in its integrated and completed form, supports my proposed definition of evolution. I believe that even according to the Biblical narrative, evolution is an integrated and progressing sense of responsible connection. The constructivist-developmental framework of spiritual growth is deeply reliant upon and informed by this comprehensive definition of spiritual evolution.

3

The Theory of Growth

When I was much younger, I had a great number of expectations for what I thought were vital components of a close personal relationship. These expectations affected my life very deeply because, at a time when I felt as though I was searching for someone who could be my wife, they exerted untold influences on the direction of my relationships, often limiting my vision and increasing my self-righteousness. I was a young and opinionated man, who desperately wanted to create a nurturing, comfortable, and loving environment for himself, as he looked into his future. There was, of course, a problem with these expectations: they brought untold trial to my budding sensibilities and consciousness as I met many a girl that could not live up to my legendary standards. This all to came to a head in one year when I was seeing a wonderful girl who, despite her understandable inability to satisfy my unreasonable demands, managed to keep my interest and overcome my desire to retreat and search elsewhere. As such, I found myself in a deep quandary: should I choose my expectations (which I still wholeheartedly believed were correct) or do I choose the girl (whom I loved dearly and whom I did not want to leave)? The prospect of choosing my expectations amounted to losing this girl. This prospect of abandoning my expectations amount to a loss of my very self, since I was unsure who I would become without my expectations. The dilemma was excruciating, and was one that lasted for almost two years.

During that period, I questioned everything I knew of myself, everything I believed I was entitled to, everything I was told I 'deserved', everything that I had originally hoped for. It was a period of intense introspection and pain, a period of literally feeling like I wasn't myself anymore, a period of feeling unhinged from the course I had set for myself. And then, one day, like a flash of insight, it happened: I found the answer, and my swirling countenance began to settle. The answer was elusively simple and deeply upsetting all at once—an answer that, since then, I have realized that all people must hear at some point in their maturation. The answer said the following: 'Time has passed. You are grown. You are no longer a child, you are now a man. All of these entitlements are those of a little boy needing to be loved, a demanding and attention seeking child. Should you want to be the man you are growing into, you have to nurture the little boy and place him in dialogue with the emerging grown man. You have to relinquish the child's fantasies (that were always nothing other than fantasies) and seek the true incarnation of your happiness. You are no longer a boy, and you should not want to remain a boy. You are grown. You must own your responsibility. You must become a man'.

Since this event in my life, I have come to know many a person who found himself or herself confronted with the same startling and often saddening realization, the same relinquishing of innocence as a price for greater wisdom and maturity, the same dose of realism as a ransom to self-responsibility and autonomy. In all cases I have encountered, the experience has been perceived as nothing less than a deep personal, and identity-threatening crisis—a crisis that ended in a fundamental re-balancing, a qualitative re-definition of how the world is viewed, interpreted, and experienced. And yet, what is missing from each person's account are the actual mechanics of this crisis-induced growth. These mechanics take place outside of our conscious awareness. Hence, the question remains very salient: How is it that human beings evolve through crises, through successive stages of spirituality and grow into higher states of maturity?

We have now laid the groundwork necessary for a more complete understanding of the constructivist-developmental framework of spiritual growth. One of the main arguments of this book is that human growth is an evolution of consciousness which gives rise to spirituality and thus the personal levels of thought, affect, and relationship. We also stated that this ground is the founding element of meaning-constitutive consciousness. So far, we have discussed the elements of spirituality, meaning, and evolution.[1] As such, we are left with the crux of the mat-

---

1. Spirituality is defined as a dynamic state of consciousness concerned with life's meaning and coherence; meaning is defined as constructed information that informs spirituality; and evolution is defined as an integrated and progressing sense of respon-

ter: what is the actual process of human growth? The purpose of this section is to outline the art and science of human consciousness development and thereby demonstrate that human growth evolves through constructed and developing processes, which come about through a process I refer to as Emergence.

SUBSTANCE: PHILOSOPHY—THE ART OF CONSCIOUSNESS

Before we can delve into the mechanical analysis provided by science, I believe that we must have a firm grounding in the generalized framework in which the processes of spiritual growth take place. In other words, before we delve into the 'how' of the progression of spiritual growth, we must gain an understanding of the 'what' and the 'why'. As such, we will develop a 'big picture' framework within which to place the scientific mechanical intricacies. It is the purpose of this section to outline some of the main lines of thought regarding the philosophy of the growth of consciousness. Our discussion will culminate in the elucidation of the Hegelian concept of 'Absolute Spirit'—the formulation of a consciousness that is aware of its environmental surround as a product of its own constructions.

The Hegelian formulation of 'Self', or 'Selfhood', is the inspiration from which the concept of a personal mode of meaning-making springs.[2] Interestingly, even though this philosophy was propounded centuries before the advent of the constructivist-developmental framework, its analysis is consistent with our phenomenological/meta-phenomenological description of 'Self'. In line with this psychological theory of Self, the Hegelian school of philosophy has stated that a mature person is more than simply a differentiated individual. This person has crossed the threshold of increased consciousness and self-consciousness, and as a result of this process, has achieved a higher and qualitatively different perspective on the world. This new perspective on the world facilitates the development of greater *integration*—of the Self with the external world, and of the Self with the various elements internal to it—of the Self with whole of its existence. For instance, as I weathered my identity-threatening crisis related to my expectations of relationships, I came to

---

sible connectedness.

2. Kegan, *The Evolving Self*, 1; de Chardin, *The Phenomenon of Man*, 19; Scruton et al, *German Philosophers*, 62; Brown, *On Hegel*, 3; Malone and Malone, *The Windows of Experience*.

understand myself more congruently, to further integrate myself into the fabric of my relations and my world, and to re-vision my future in a manner consistent with my evolution and development. It is in light of this mode of thought that de Chardin stated that a Self is an organism that has transcended individuality and has thereby attained Selfhood.[3] In other words, the Self is that entity which has transcended the exclusive grasp on the 'Me' and has relinquished its growth to the guidance of the 'I'. The congruent combination of the 'I' and the 'Me' is called Selfhood. Since the attainment of Selfhood has proven essential to the success of humanity's past and present evolution, I believe that its fuller attainment must be an essential aim for the personal evolutionary efforts of Spiritual Leaders. This matter of the pre-eminent Self, since it involves and penetrates the entire person, is for me not simply a matter of philosophy and spirituality, but more specifically, a matter of spirituality supported by the honest inquiry of philosophical and psychological knowledge. Consequently, a partnering force to the pivotal role of spirituality is the fluid process of meaning-making, which informs and undergirds spirituality. This counter-balance of science and spirituality prevents the focus of spiritual growth from being diluted and rooted in the empirical world alone, while simultaneously ensuring that the doctrine does not fall into a rhapsodized account of spiritual illumination. In addition, the integration of spirituality into the framework of growth brings with it the essential dimension of the pursuit of connectedness. As such, we begin to appreciate a fuller concept of reality as a series of interrelations in which humanity actively participates. It is to this idea that Lonergan speaks when he points out that the appearance of a human Self is the culmination of two distinct trends: the trend toward a more stringent individualization (responsibility and autonomy), and the complementary trend toward greater interrelation and cooperation (connectedness).[4] In other words, a Self is an individual who transcends mere individuality in the act of conscious participation in the world. But, by what road is this Self achieved? What evolutionary process takes place that fosters the broadening of our meaning-making?

The answer to this question lies in the elucidation of how human consciousness grasps its conceptions of reality. When humanity begins to interact with its environment, it inevitably places itself at the cen-

---

3. de Chardin, *The Phenomenon of Man*, 21.
4. Lonergan, *Insight*, 162.

ter of its perceptions as it makes meaning.[5] That is, we have an innate tendency to infuse our perceptions with nuances of what we believe to be pure objectivity. I have sat innumerable times in a counseling office and listened to both members of a couple relate the same story to me from their respective points of view, each staunchly stipulating their conviction that their version of the story is the true and more 'objective' version. Consequently, we separate ourselves from whatever it is we are observing. To provide another example, science often falls prey to the belief that a person can observe a phenomenon in the same form that it would take place in his or her absence. Instinctively, many scientists go to work as if they could stare down from a great height, penetrate the world with their consciousness, and walk away without having somehow affected or influenced what they had observed. It is my contention that we are inclined to isolate ourselves from things, events, experiences, and beings which surround us, as though we were looking at them from the outside, from the shelter of an impenetrable observatory. That is, I believe that we too easily act as if we are mere spectators to life, rather than elements of the life that pushes us all forward. As spectators, we render ourselves incapable of observing and experiencing our own participation and agency in the events and complexities of our lives. It is my belief that this form of experiential separation amounts to a virtual alienation of the developing consciousness from its very actions within the environmental surround and, thus, forms an effective block to Hegelian and Loneranganian, as well as to our phenomenological/meta-phenomenological conceptions of Self. As such, non-participation in the things, events, experiences and beings we encounter, as exemplified by our innate tendency to try to apprehend the nature of reality by using our consciousness as nothing other than a grasping tool, constitutes a tacit and effective distancing of the evolving consciousness from the very source of its meaning—personal engagement in the quest for and experience of reality.[6]

---

5. For more on this phenomenon, please see Malone and Malone, *The Windows of Experience* and de Chardin, *The Phenomenon of Man*, Coppleston, *On John Locke*, Seobock, *The Tell-Tale Sign*, Pierce, *Collected Works*.

6. The lack of personal engagement was the primary reason for rejecting atomism as a viable approach to Biblical discourse (for our purposes), and adhering to a narrative theological method. As such, in this context, we have the philosophical analogue to our theological methodology.

In assuming this distant stance, we are immediately beset by insurmountable worries. If trying to know reality involves the process of using our consciousness to grasp reality, is there truly no danger that the simple application of our consciousness to the task does not, in and of itself, alter what it is we finally end up grasping? Hegel answers this paramount query by explaining that even if we regard our consciousness as the passive medium through which we observe and attempt to grasp reality, we are still in fact observing reality through the sieve of a medium. We can never know reality itself, devoid of our consciousness.[7] Therefore, in an ironically circular construction, Hegel believes that the application of our consciousness leaves a deep and indelible mark on the perceptions we assimilate into consciousness. This is nothing other than the philosophical incarnation of the process of meaning-making. It is to these modified perceptions that we react as we evolve our budding spirituality. Many psychotherapists and pastoral counselors are echoing Hegel's salient words by illuminating the realization that even in the most objective of scientific pursuits, practitioners are inadvertently steeped in the conventions they adopted in the course of their personal and professional development. In light of this, when they reach the conclusion of their analyses, practitioners may be humbled and frustrated by the difficulty they find in extruding with any certainty whether the structure they have reached is the actual essence of the matter they are studying, or whether they are experiencing reflections of their own preferences. Through this inextricable process of discerning meaning, subject (the observer's activity of perceiving) and object (the observer's conscious apprehensions) marry and mutually transform each other in the very personal act of knowing. As a consequence, every act of knowing carries within it the elements of the tacit subject and the externalized object. The intertwining of these elements is that which is often left out of the observer's conscious apprehension of his or her knowing. But what happens, in the idealized situation, when a Self develops to a plane where its vision is not limited to its own vantage point but is able to coincide its subjectivity to match the way the universe is objectively distributed? I believe that at this point, vision moves toward its zenith, meaning reaches its crowning heights. Humanity sees, evolves, and integrates. In my opinion, herein lies the fundamental definition of the movement of consciousness.

7. Scruton, et al, *German Philosophers,* 166.

Analogous to the development of the Self, the elements of consciousness complicate and differentiate their nature with the passage of time. In light of this, many developmental scholars believe that consciousness displays itself as a shifting canvas of awareness, a series of evolutions, whose former stages are engulfed and transformed (integrated) into later stages. As such, each level of consciousness conceives of reality according to its particular level of awareness. It is this concept that Hegelian philosophy addresses when it denies the existence of a single truth. According to Hegel, each individual truth is part of a whole process of transformation.[8] Hence, what is important is not the single truth itself, but rather the continuous *movement* of consciousness through its unique evolutions and its conceptions of truth. Similarly, what is important is not the specific incarnations of meaning perceived by an individual, but rather the sequence of transformational evolutions undergone by the individual's meaning-making over time. In Hegel's own words:

> Judged by that movement, the particular shapes which consciousness assumes do not indeed subsist any more than do the determinant thoughts and ideas, but they are all the same—as much positive and necessary movement as they are negative and transitory.[9]

The essence of this form of movement is what Hegel attributes to the Absolute Spirit.

Hegel, then, has set himself a Herculean task. Starting with a powerful critique of the dualism of Kantian thought, he sets out to develop a new method. This method is to trace the progressive development of all possible forms of consciousness to the final goal of genuine knowledge.[10] This is not the knowledge of the appearance of reality but rather of reality as it truly is.[11] As such, his expansive conception of consciousness is not limited to the cognitive. Rather, it is the prior ground from which the cognitive springs—the same ground that gives birth to the affective and the relational. This act, this process through which our evolving consciousness and progressing meaning moves through a process of

8. Brown, *On Hegel*, 52.
9. Hegel in Brown, *On Hegel*, 52.
10. A discussion that is still taking place today in Christian circles. For more, please see Wolterstorff, *Reason*; Bellous, *Educating Faith*; Misak, *Truth*.
11. Scruton, et al, *German Philosophers*, 170.

complexification and penetrates further into the objective and the transcendent aspects of life, I will call the 'Process of Emergence'.[12]

Emergence can be further defined as the process by which humanity progresses by slowly elaborating the essence and the totality of the Creation deposited within and around it.[13] This grand process of evolution, I believe, is the basis for the materialization of the Self, the foundation of the progressive spiritualization of all of humanity. Within the crises arising from life and reflection, the next stage of evolution of Self emerges. The former disposition is absorbed into the higher consciousness.[14] With that very ability, humanity bursts forth upon the stages of the empirical universe and of God's Holy Creation. It transcends the mundane niches into which objects are classified and introduces and new epoch. It is through the Holy process of humanity's self-conscious Emergence that meaning is given a new skin and, as such, finds its soul.

But what of this self-conscious aspect? Hegel clearly states that self-consciousness is held firmly within the progression of Emergence, and is a vital step in the development of the Absolute Spirit.[15] The instrument of self-consciousness he calls 'reflection', where reflection is the power acquired by a consciousness to turn upon itself, to take possession of itself as an object to itself, with its own consistency and value. In the words of de Chardin: "No longer merely to know, but to know oneself; no longer merely to know, but to know that one knows."[16] Therefore, by this individualization of oneself within the depths of oneself, the human who was once fused with a diffuse circle of undifferentiated perceptions and activities emerges as a new focal point, through which the experiences of the perceptions and activities are pulled together into a subjectivity that is conscious of its own organization of meaning. Thus, we come to a central theme in Hegelian philosophy: the consciousness of an infinitely rich unity of thought and reality, of form and content, is effected through the challenge of the crises of life, as perceived through

12. Whereas evolution is the unfolding of a possibility, an integrated and progressive sense of responsible connectedness, Emergence (a more specific term, and a form of evolution in itself) is the movement of a consciousness out of the 'merge', of moving from levels of a fused subjectivity to levels of greater differentiation and integration into life's interconnections.
13. de Chardin, *The Phenomenon of Man,* 181.
14. Brown, *On Hegel,* 56.
15. Hegel in Scruton, et al, *German Philosophers,* 173.
16. de Chardin, *The Phenomenon of Man,* 165.

self-consciousness. Since every conflict is a relational process between what is Self and what is Other, Emergence progresses by naming and transcending the one-sided terms that have come into conflict.[17] It is through the process of Emergence, then, that we become critically aware of Absolute Spirit.

Our final task, then, is to examine what Hegel meant by his concept of Absolute Spirit. As we have already stated, the Hegelian view holds that objects are not things existing independent of consciousness, but rather are interpretations of consciousness, as it perceives its world. In other words, objects are constructed harbingers of meaning for each individual. At the level of self-consciousness, humanity becomes aware of the laws of the universe as laws of its own creation and, therefore, for the first time, consciousness now has itself as the object of its scrutiny. It is at this stage that consciousness begins to shape the world practically as well as intellectually.[18] Consciousness, thus, begins to interpret and affect its internal, spiritual, and social worlds. That is, in the words of Scruton, "although humanity may set out to track the path of consciousness as it comes to know reality, at the end of the road it finds that it has been watching its consciousness as it *constructs* reality."[19] To Hegel, then, Absolute Spirit is reached when consciousness becomes aware that there is *nothing to be grasped* beyond itself, that it is united with what it is grasping. Absolute Spirit is consciousness achieving awareness of itself in the shape of consciousness.[20] Hegel said: "The truth is the whole, but the whole is only the essence of perfecting itself through self-conscious development."[21] In light of Hegel's view of Absolute Spirit, it becomes clear that the notion of the whole is not to be grasped as a dimension of Being—a static state implying existence and presence. Rather, it is fundamentally to be understood as the basis of the transformational concept of Becoming.

Life, being an ascent of consciousness and meaning, advances by transforming and re-transforming itself in its very depths. Through Emergence and in response to life's constant and unabating challenges, consciousness has to constantly become different from its current con-

17. Lefebvre, *Dialectical Materialism*, 25.
18. Scruton, et al, *German Philosophers*, 185.
19. Scruton, et al, *German Philosophers*, 189.
20. Hegel in Scruton, et al, *German Philosophers*, 189.
21. Hegel in Brown, *On Hegel*, 54.

structed incarnation so as to unwaveringly remain an integrous Self. Because this phenomenon takes place within our Selves, it is a process that is accessible to our apprehension. It is through access to such clarity that our vision expands and allows us to see the further advances of consciousness. Also, the further an emergent self-consciousness arises from the anonymous masses of subjectivity, the greater becomes the force within it that can be stored up and transmitted by means of example and education.

Humanity then is the center of its own perception and at the same time, the center of construction of the empirical Universe and of God's Holy Creation. If to seek is really to become more, if vision is really fuller Selfhood, then we become aware of the paradoxical and ironic situation of our existence: throughout our existence, we become aware that we are the players, we are the cards being played, and we are the stakes. Nothing can go on if we choose to leave the table. And yet, no power forces us to remain.[22]

SUBSTANCE: PSYCHOLOGY—THE SCIENCE OF CONSCIOUSNESS

The philosophical discussion above outlines a way in which humanity can be seen and studied as a phenomenon: a process to be described and analyzed. Since the progression of human consciousness is a form of evolution, I do not believe that it can be described or evaluated solely on the basis of its origins (psychological geneticism). As such, I contend that human consciousness must be defined by its direction, by its limitations, and by its potential and dynamic trends.

Ever since the colonization of the New World, Western culture has tended toward an ethic of individualism and autonomy. We are constantly bombarded with messages about growing up and out of contexts, of standing on our own two feet, of achieving a state of independent thought (which most often finds expression in a staunchly self-assertive, self-centered, and uncooperative demeanor). In these pages, however, I am aligning with many humanistic philosophers, psychologists and theologians in stating that the attainment of a state of independence is *not* the greatest notion of maturity. In other words, I believe that a highly differentiated psychological autonomy is not automatically equated with

---

22. de Chardin, *The Phenomenon of Man*, 15.

the pinnacle of human evolution. There is an alternative to this particular view that I believe is more balanced, more emergent, and more in line with the spiritual tenets of the Judeo-Christian inheritance. The conception I will discuss below does not discard differentiated autonomy (a conception devoid of autonomy and differentiation would risk drowning the unanchored Self in a sea of social exigencies) but rather subsumes it to a larger theory of apprehension. This theory is called the constructivist-developmental theory of spiritual growth.

The constructivist-developmental theory of spiritual growth is fundamentally a humanistic and psychodynamic approach, uniquely well-suited to studying and categorizing the processes of spiritual evolution. As such, it is mainly focused on determining norms of spiritual health that are both universal and dynamic. To be concerned with norms that are universal is a daunting task, to say the least. In order to be successful in this endeavor, constructivist-developmentalism focuses its efforts on an underlying tenet of human ontology and on the ground from which spirituality springs—meaning-making and its incarnations through the lifecycle. In addition, constructivist-developmentalism treats spiritual health as a dynamic, ever-moving, ever-progressing unfolding of spirit. As such, at no point does the framework perceive static and stabilized structures as anything other than a brief respite on the road to continuous and inescapable evolution. Thus, constructivist-developmentalism is uniquely tailored to addressing our concern with the mechanics and promotion of growth and Emergence, as they are applied to our human spiritual health. It is not, therefore, a diagnostic model from which to simply label aberrations or identify illnesses. Although the discovery of personal maladjustment can take place through its powerful insights, constructivist-developmentalism is rather a discipline of empowerment, a challenging and probing companionship, and an insight into humanity's very soul. In today's therapeutic climate, we are no longer seeing the once legendary battle between the traditionally medico-diagnostic and the humanistic approaches to care. In fact, humanistic approaches have concretized their ascendancy and are now being taught and mentored as crucial and founding care giving techniques, especially in pastoral care circles. And yet, even these humanistic approaches often lack a dimension of univeralism or dynamism—they are often culturally embedded, 'client as *fait accompli*' approaches that do not attend to what I believe is the grounding process of our development: the process of Emergence.

As a foundation to our understanding of the complexities of the constructivist-developmental framework, I believe a few additional words about the psychological milieu would be useful.

Because of their unique and particular constructions, different schools of thought will categorize frameworks of psychological approaches in their own unique ways. These conceptions are usually based on the fundamental drivers of therapeutic engagement of each of these schools, such as direction vs. non-direction, emotive vs. cognitive, or biological vs. theological. With respect to the constructivist-developmental approach to healing, the dyad can be defined as entity vs. process. If such a lens to viewing history is adopted, we find that the two traditions that have had the greatest impact on our developmental climate are the classical psychoanalytic tradition (begun by Sigmund Freud), and the existential-phenomenological tradition (championed by Carl Rogers).[23] In piecing together a more holistic psychological approach, I find that constructive-developmentalism does a great deal of honor to the deep convictions of these traditions, while simultaneously building on their shortcomings.

The classical psychoanalytical school focuses most of its energy on the 'biological system' that is within us and that fundamentally and unwittingly affects our behaviors and drives. Being conceived during a very mechanistic period in scientific epistemology, the psychoanalytic framework was primarily concerned with the accretion and release of particular internal biological drives, as well as the human desire to avoid the pain that this internal interplay evokes. As such, the psychoanalytic tradition can be likened to a therapeutic version of Newton's laws of thermodynamics, where energy is continually transferred and where every energetic action produces an opposing and countervailing reaction. The classical tradition views the individual 'ego' as primarily motivated by the desires to reduce or eliminate unpleasurable aspects in life. The 'ego', the concept associated with personality, is therefore at the mercy of the conflicting and confounding opposing forces which exert influence from below and from above. Below the 'ego' resides the infamous 'id'— a hotbed of instinctual and seminal desires associated with biological drives. Above the 'ego' is the ephemeral 'superego'—a monitoring force within the psyche that functions in a quasi-conscience fashion. As a re-

---

23. Kegan juxtaposes these two schools of thought throughout his works. For more, please see Kegan, *The Evolving Self,* and *In Over Our Heads.*

sult of this schema, the mentally or emotionally ill individual is thought to turn away from the 'ego' because the internal system of warding off displeasure caused by the conflict of id and superego has somehow broken down.

The psychoanalytic tradition, despite current voices decrying its alleged abuses of care seekers, has positive characteristics to commend it. First, it was Freud and his followers, the creators of this tradition, that are generally accredited with making psychotherapy a recognized and respected field in the healing sector. Far from a world of mysterious potions and dubious mental diagnoses, the psychoanalytic tradition gave a vocabulary and outlook of mental distress that was universal and treatable—a bias that is still alive and well today. Second, the tradition highlighted the importance of our physical-ness, our biology. I often find that many care-givers, counselors, and therapists even today underestimate the role our very bodies and instincts play in our spiritual and mental constructions. And third, it encouraged many generations of theorists and therapists to innovate conceptions of human apprehension, resulting in such growthful disciplines as object relations and internal representation formulations (which today are incorporated into the study of meaning-making). And yet, Freud's legacy presents some shortcomings.

In my opinion, psychoanalytic theory suffers from a view of biology that is outdated and narrow. It is true that biological drives have been shown to be linked to the experience of daily living, to the mitigating of affect, to the determination of the complexity of thought, and to metaphors of spiritual processes. Recent scientific endeavors, however, have concluded against the proposition of biology as the determinative and ultimate aspect of human consciousness.[24] In addition, although psychoanalytic theory accedes to the existence of subject-object relations, it places these relations firmly in the external realm. In other words, this school of thought suffers from the one-sided tendency to overlook the dimensions of the Self that are consciously participative in the activities of life.

On the other side of the coin, we find the countervailing influences of the existential-phenomenological tradition. In the 1950s and 1960s, Carl Rogers' client-centered counseling approach fundamentally re-

---

24. Please see Goleman, *Emotional Intelligence*; Kohut, *The Analysis of Self*; Bollas, *The Shadow of the Object*; and Antony, *Skills in Counseling*.

oriented the practice of care-giving and, today, is still the primary mode of therapeutic relating in pastoral circles. As such, because of its very great influence, it is essential for us to both incorporate its strengths into our discussion of constructivist-developmental Spiritual Leadership, but also to remain keenly aware of the pitfalls it presents.

In contrast to earlier Freudian conceptions of the human person, Rogers conceived of what he felt was an intrinsic process of transformation and development. His first principle was the Actualizing Tendency: the inherent tendency of the organism to develop all its capacities in ways which serve or enhance its existence. The Tendency did not only meet deficiency needs, but also promoted a development toward differentiation, toward the expansion of growth, and toward the expansion of personal effectiveness. It is differentiated growth toward autonomy and away from heteronomy (the placement of the center of personal power outside oneself).[25] As such, Rogers' conception involved the belief that individual and environmental surround are inextricably linked in a constant dialectic—one which is capitalized upon by a struggling subjectivity as it works to differentiate and find autonomous authority. Thus, in the words of Kegan, Rogers seems to label the Actualizing Tendency as

> the sole motive of personality; there are no separate systems with motives of their own. There is presumed to be a basic unity to personality, a unity best understood as a process rather than as an entity. This process, according to Rogers' conception, gives rise to the 'self', the meaning-making system with which the process gets identified. Anxiety, defense, and psychological maladjustment are all understood in the context of the efforts to maintain the Self-system.[26]

It is clear that this system of therapy has many positive aspects to uphold it. First, it provides a framework from which to liberate the human subjectivity from the autonomous and biologically-driven motivations of Freudian thought; second, it focuses on the individual as process rather than on the individual as static equilibrium, thereby re-orienting the focus of therapy from healing illness to promoting growth; third, it empowers the individual to work toward the achievement and furtherance of the 'Self', a deeply held congruence of the various levels of being; and fourth, it brings care-givers down from the traditionally high pedes-

---

25. I am here liberally paraphrasing Rogers, *Client-Centered Therapy*, 196.
26. Kegan, *The Evolving Self*, 5.

tal on which they were placed, and permits them to co-mingle as a peer part of the therapeutic relationship. And yet, as with the classical psychoanalytic approach, with respect to constructivist-developmentalism, there are some strong reservations evoked by the Rogerian system.

In spite of its clear warmth and respect for the agency of each person, two important reservations regarding its application require some attention. First, Rogers' conception deals with the client as presented in the counseling room. As such, narratives and meanings are taken as they are presented by the care seeker and used in their current form to inform the therapeutic process. I believe, therefore, that the Rogerian framework is present-focused in its approach, effectively taking the presenting client as a completed product, rather than as the very motion of spiritual development. As a result, made meanings are given ascendancy over transforming meanings, thereby potentially disengaging the current construction of meaning-making from any that might arise through spiritual movement. As such, a developmental lifecycle plotline is not elucidated through the helping relationship, cheating the counselor of potentially crucial information that could be used to forge a deep and constructive joining with the client.

Second, Rogers' bias is harmonious with that of Western culture mentioned above—he was predominantly concerned with differentiation and autonomy. Although I have no reservations on stipulating the importance of differentiation from an environmental surround, what is more important, from a constructivist-developmental point of view, is the combination of differentiation with its complementary process of integration. Devoid one or the other, a psychotherapeutic framework tips itself off-balance and cheats the client and counselor from having a grounded view of the possible courses of consciousness development.

To my mind, the primary concern with either of these frameworks is their lack of ability to attend to the spiritual formation of humanity, as that formation spans and integrates *both* the concepts of the Internal (the construction and process of the Self) and External (the role of environment, instinct, and biology), the role of the static as well as the role of movement, the concepts of the cognitive, affective, and relational, the concepts of differentiation *and* integration—in other words, the combined foundations of the process of meaning-making and spiritual growth. The constructivist-developmental framework, however, attends to these very things. As such, it is uniquely useful for an understanding of and deeply concerned with the movement of spirituality, the mechanics of meaning-making, the growth of consciousness, and the furtherance of evolution—in short, the spiritual development of a healthy and integrated Self. Daniel Stern, in describing the growth and transformation of young children, highlighted the existence of ever-more complex organizations and reorganizations of an emerging 'Self'. Barnet and Barnet summarize Stern's viewpoints by saying that he believed that the 'Self' is an agent of action, an experiencer of feelings, a maker of intentions, an architect of plans, a communicator, and a sharer of personal knowledge.[27] As such, a 'Self' is here understood to refer as much to the activity of meaning-making and on-going, perpetual evolution as it does to the physical entity. This maturity of the Self, as achieved through perceptual evolution, would be the very subject of our new psychological theory. Thus, the constructivist-developmental concept of the spiritual growth of the 'Self' is the subject of this book.

Subject-Object Theory

Having set the psychological stage for the introduction of a comprehensive theory that addresses the complexities of spirituality, meaning, and evolution, I will now discuss the mechanical precursor of the constructivist-developmental scheme for spiritual growth: Subject-Object theory. This is the last stage of investigation required before discussing the actual theory itself.

According to Kegan, 'object' refers to those elements of our knowing or organizing that we can "reflect on, handle, look at, perceive, be responsible for, relate to each other, take control of, internalize, assimilate, or otherwise operate on." All these characteristics highlight the fact that the elements of current knowing are not the whole of who we are.[28] They are elements that are distinct enough from us that we can recognize them and do something about them, having emerged from a state of fusion with them.

'Subject' refers to those elements of our knowing or organizing with which we identify ourselves, to which we tie ourselves, with which we are fused, in which we are embedded.[29] In Kegan's words:

---

27. Stern in Barnet and Barnet, *The Youngest Minds*, 150.
28. Kegan, *The Evolving Self*, 32.
29. Kegan, *The Evolving Self*, 32.

> Object speaks to that which some motion has made separate or distinct from the Self. In addition, 'object' is separate and distinct from its own motion... We cannot be responsible for, in control of, or effectual upon that which is subject [since it is fused with our identity]. Subject is immediate; object is mediate. Subject is ultimate or absolute; object is relative.[30]

Subject-Object theory, by this line of reasoning, has to do with our relationship to those elements that the movement of Emergence has unfused from our subjectivity, has made separate from us, and has added to our repertoire of external entities. Our experience of growth is held within the process and dynamics of this separation itself. Therefore, as Kegan states, objects are known only through the lens of the subject, and the subject can come to know itself only by acting on objects, whether the action is material, cognitive, affective, social, or spiritual.[31]

According to Subject-Object theory, the process of human evolution involves an increase in vision through the refinement of the Subject, and the very creation of new Objects.[32] In this creation, we distance ourselves from the Object and stand apart from it and therefore undergo a transformative differentiation (Subject refinement). In other words, by separating from that which we now perceive as 'not me', we refine our sense of Self, emerge from a fusion with externals that once confounded our perceptions, and develop a purer, more integrous, more cohesive, and better apprehended Self. In contradistinction to this process, by creating the Object and standing apart from it, we have created a strange duality in our understanding. This duality is not a tenable spiritual state, since holding something at a constant distance from consciousness requires the outlay of considerable energy. As such, in light of the fact that we can now literally perceive that which was once hidden to us (the new Object), we can choose to incorporate this new Object into our conceptions of reality, and therefore, for the first time, enter into a relationship with it (hence, Subject-Object relations). As such, this creative process brings together the two poles of person and environment, of differentiation and integration, effectively bridging this mysterious dialectic, and results in the evolution of meaning and the progression of Emergence.[33]

---

30. Kegan, *The Evolving Self*, 12.
31. Kegan, *The Evolving Self*, 77.
32. Kegan, *The Evolving Self*, 77.
33. Kegan, *In Over Our Heads*, 34.; _____, *Evolving Self*, 8.

As an example, let us examine a single act of Objectification in the life of an infant. Child psychologists generally agree that the state of infancy is a state of complete unity with the world. The infant does not perceive a distinction between itself and its caretakers or surroundings. As such, everything that comes into the infant's frame of experience is interpreted as an extension of itself. In constructivist-developmental language, the infant is embedded in a state of all-encompassing Subject since everything is tied to its own identity. There is no Object in the infant's world because there is only the infant itself. As such, everything perceived in the experiential field of the child is filed away as the action and influence of the all-pervasive Subject—that with which the child is fused.

One day, however, this changes. As the baby is happily swiping at the air in front of her face with her hand, she begins to perceive for the first time, that she might be able to control that which is doing the swiping. As a consequence, she has learned an important lesson. She *is* not her hand—her hand is no longer part of her identity. Rather, she *has* a hand—it is something she can perceive as 'not me'. And, in addition to this wondrous discovery, she learns that she can cause the hand to work on the world around her. She is in control of the hand and can now will it to operate. These are the very actions that we are discussing in the Subject-Object balance. As the infant comes to realize that her hand is something she has and not something she is, her Subject comes to the realization that her hand is an Object to her. As such, her former Subjectivity is challenged and reshaped by the discovery. Her new Subject is now everything that was in the old Subject, minus her hand. Consequently, since the hand is now something that is separate from her, she can for the first time relate to it, and integrate it into her conception of the world. In relation to her newly found Object, she discovers that she is the boss, the owner, and the controller of this new Object. Although this example of Object creation may appear basic, it is the very action through which the process occurs for the remainder of spiritual evolution—even though the elements of the individual's experience that are set apart as Objects increase in subtlety and finesse throughout life.

Consequently, Subject-Object theory dares to imagine a Hegelian lifelong process of development: a succession of qualitative differentiations of the Self from embeddedness in the world, in which there arises a qualitatively different object with which to be in relation.[34] The term

---

34. Please see Scruton, et al, *German Philosophers*, 60; see also Kegan, 73–85, in

Subject-Object theory engenders the capability of the person to recognize (literally, to re-know) that another individual may be different, not only in terms of the distinctness of the Self, but also in the very construction of how that person conceives of his or her distinctness from the world. Each new principle of emergent organization differs in terms of what is subject and what is object. Every principle of meaning is constituted by a subject-object relationship. In the case of classical psychoanalytic theory, the events of earlier life are taken as fundamentally determinative of the problems in later life. In Subject-Object theory, what is taken as fundamental is the very *activity* of meaning constitutive evolution, which persists throughout all of life.

As seen through this description, then, Subject-Object theory fulfills the countervailing requirements we listed above: it engages the scientific and the faithful, it undergirds the cognitive, affective, social, and spiritual aspects of life as the prior ground of motivation; it attends to the shape of our various consolidations of meaning and the universal processes of constructing and reconstituting meaning; it is a process of Emergence undergirded by human evolution; it accounts for the movement of spirituality. Consequently, Subject-Object theory forms the foundational framework on which the constructivist-developmental approach to spiritual growth will be built.

The Contribution of Piaget

We have discussed the concept that growth is brought about through the creation of Objects from emerging Subjects. This section, drawing on the seminal work of Jean Piaget, will describe the method through which Objects are created by Subjects.

Jean Piaget offers a developmental theory specifically intended to demonstrate how the intellectual construction of the mature formal stages of being begins in the sensorimotor structures of infancy, continues through several stages, and reaches its zenith in the abstract logical structures of formal cognitive operations. It is an evolution not of the absence of knowledge to its presence, but rather of the transformation of knowledge from inferior states to superior sophistication. Although the details of the stages presented by Piaget have come under critical scrutiny in recent years, the method by which his debated stages prog-

---

which there is an excellent account of how this related to other psychoanalytic and therapeutic frameworks.

ress is very salient, and widely accepted as a mechanism of development. His characteristic method of argument is dialectical and he often refers to his method as 'dialectical constructionism'. Intrinsic to his dialectical thought is the Aristotelian counterbalance of 'Thesis' and 'Antithesis'.

Following the general model set forth by Aristotle, Piaget argued that there is always a construction, the 'Thesis', which has somehow come into contradiction with some element of reality, the 'Antithesis'. The resolution of the 'Thesis' and the 'Antithesis' results in a qualitative re-cognizing of the relationship between them, and thus a more evolved consciousness of reality. This new consciousness, which resolves the 'Thesis-Antithesis' conflict, Piaget calls the 'Synthesis'.[35] As an example, we can think of a situation in which a particular student deeply admires and respects a mentor that she has—this construction is analogous to the Thesis. Over time, however, she comes to see that that mentor has flaws that she did not anticipate—flaws that are intense enough to cause her admiration of him to be called into serious question (this is the Antithesis). Through a desire not to lose the mentor who has meant so much in her life, the student is now confronted with a grueling crisis: how can she maintain her admiration for the mentor in light of these arising flaws? Her solution, after a lengthy internal struggle no doubt (anyone who has undergone such a challenge can attest to the far-reaching personal implications of such a crisis), is to conceive of her mentor no longer in the aggrandized fashion of which she is accustomed, but to come to see him as a truly remarkable man—a man who, although he has strengths and wisdom to share with her, is just as fallen a human as she. This is a fundamental re-definition of the concept she held of her mentor, a concept that manages to span the considerable gap between the Thesis and the Antithesis while rendering a solution that transcends both sides of the duality. It is a concept that has a more congruent alignment with the truth, and is therefore, a more constructive viewpoint for the student to hold. This conclusion is the Synthesis.

As such, although each synthesis transcends its prior predecessors, it retains their insights and avoids their conceptual limitations. The development of the Synthesis, therefore, is not a function of linear deductive reasoning, an agglomeration of premises, or the strategic re-conception of conflicting patterns in order to cognitively resolve disjunction. Rather the development of the Synthesis is the qualitative re-definition of the

35. Richmond, *Piaget*, 6.

very terms of each side of the Thesis-Antithesis equation, a re-definition that effects a fundamentally different, fuller, and more congruent apprehension of the terms of the presented reality—a greater knowing and a more insightful vision. Yet, although Synthesis is the creation of a heightened knowing and the development of higher qualitative apprehensions, it is not stable in the absolute sense. As such, Synthesis, once established, becomes the new Thesis for the groping consciousness and is susceptible to the attacks of later Antitheses. Synthesis, therefore, is a shining example of the engine of a process that conforms to Hegel's ever-progressive motion.

The Thesis is reflective of the current structure of meaning-making mastered by the individual, whereas the Antithesis presents a creative force which challenges the current structure and demands accommodation.[36] According to Boden, in each case, the 'Thesis' posits structure without genesis, and the 'Antithesis' posits genesis without structure. Synthesis, in turn, provides genesis with structure, a germinal structuralization, which focuses on the development of increasingly equilibrated structures.[37] Scholars such as William Perry, Lawrence Kohlberg, Erik Erickson, Robert Kegan, and James Fowler believe that this continual equilibration is central to all developmental processes.[38]

Piaget believed that Synthesis is considered and accepted through the differential processes of Assimilation and Accommodation. Assimilation is defined as a modification of an incoming stimulus by the activity of a preexistent structure.[39] In other words, Assimilation is the interpretation of incoming stimulus by our already constructed meaning system, so as to maintain internal equilibrium. For example, our student may take information about dubious behavior in which her mentor engages and choose to perceive these actions as somehow moral, attributing to him a moral acuity and judgment that is above her own

---

36. Pierce undertakers an involved elucidation of similar concepts in his account of the mechanics of semiology. According to him, there are two forces that are dominant in semiological apprehension: a force of Continuity that assimilates information into an already existing interpretive structure and a force of Chance, that topples that structure by introducing information that cannot be assimilated. The latter results in redefinition of meaning structures. For more, please see Pierce, *Collected Works*, 53–81.

37. Boden, *Piaget*, 6.

38. Perry, *College Years*, add Erikson, *Childhood and Society*, Kohlberg, *Moral Stages*, Fowler, *Stages of Faith*, Kegan, *Evolving Self*.

39. Boden, *Piaget*, 23.

and that therefore does not have to be fully understood by her. Should Assimilation not be able to exert its effect on a particular stimulus, Accommodation ensues. Accommodation is defined as the active modification of the Self-structure, so as to adapt to the new stimulus.[40] In other words, Accommodation takes place when the presenting stimulus is too incongruent to be contained within the boundaries of the current constructions of meaning, and therefore results in a complete re-definition of the meaning system to encompass the new stimulus. The result of this process is a new equilibrium (reflected in our student's redefined and more congruent conception of her mentor). Reflective of Piaget's dialectical approach, equilibrium is both a relatively stable (it subsists as a Thesis for a length of time and is infused with the determinative power of Thesis for that time), and a relatively dynamic state of the structure (since it can accept new inputs, including those that are incongruent with its posited tenets), such that it can adapt to new input (dynamic) with minimal change (static).

Since equilibrium is not perfect (and therefore not permanent), an eventual Antithetical stimulus will defeat the assimilative powers developed in the existing Thesis structure. If the Self is to deal with the tension constructively, a structural re-development of the equilibrium must take place (accommodation). As such, the process of evolutionary development to Piaget is the progression from one equilibrium to a more considered one, one in which the subject is increasingly differentiated from the object.[41] Consequently, the newly created object can now be internalized into the newly created subject. Therefore, according to Piaget and very much in harmony with Subject-Object theory, integrative internalization is the process by which something becomes *less* subjective, in which that which we have perceived as 'not-me' truly comes to be known as 'not-me', and comes to take its place among the complexities of what I perceive to be the external world (my objects). Yet, it is just this Hegelian formulation which makes Piagetian perspectives so descriptive of the processes by which subject-object relations result in consciousness development.

This development promoting movement of subject and object is referred to by Piaget as 'decentration'. Decentration is the process by which an old center of consciousness is lost, in favor of a new, more evolved

---

40. Boden, *Piaget*, 23.
41. Barnet and Barnet, *The Youngest Minds*, 45.

center. Since decentration is an evolutionary process, each emergent center better guarantees the world its distinct integrity as a newly created object.[42] It is yet another way of telling the story of the successive levels of emergence from embeddedness (differentiation), and the resultant relationship to the new emergent objects (integration).[43]

I believe that as the prior ground of the reconstructions of the Self, this evolutionary process is the unifying context for, and the very source behind thought, feeling, and personality. In arguing for evolutionary activity as the very ground of personality, constructivist-developmental theory is not choosing between aspects of cognition, affect, or socialization. In contrast to classical psychoanalytic and existential-phenomenological theories, constructivist-developmental theory focuses its attention on the *movement* of consciousness, which gives rise to all levels of Self. Harkening back to our earlier definition of spirituality, constructivist-developmental theory truly walks in the realm of spiritual evolution by delineating the progress of consciousness as it increases in meaning, coherence, responsibility and connectedness.

I can now turn my attention to the topic of constructivist-developmental theory itself.

Constructivist-Developmental Theory

So far, I have covered a wide range of interrelated topics: I have defined spirituality, evolution, and meaning as foundational aspects of the developing Self.[44] Having informed my fundamental definitions with the Biblical tradition, I located these terms within a philosophical structure of Selfhood that led to the apprehension of Hegel's Absolute Spirit.[45] Finally, I correlated the Hegelian concept of Absolute Spirit with the scientific theories of Subject-Object relations and the Piagetian concept of Assimilation-Accommodation-Decentration-Equilibrium. Going back

---

42. Kegan, *The Evolving Self,* 294; C.S. Pierce also proposed such a conception. According to him, epistemological equilibrium takes place after repeated rounds of surprise, doubt, and inquiry. Pierce, *Collected Works.*

43. Kegan, *The Evolving Self,* 31.

44. Spirituality is defined as a dynamic state of consciousness concerned with life's meaning and coherence; meaning is defined as constructed information that informs spirituality; and evolution is defined as an integrated and progressing sense of responsible connectedness.

45. Hegel's Absolute Spirit is defined as consciousness that has come to be aware of itself as consciousness.

to the original argument posited in the Prologue, we are now left with a final task in our elucidation of the 'emergence of ever-increasing forms of complexity within a person's equilibrium': the pulling together of all the pieces through a further exploration of human growth, as interpreted through the constructivist-developmental lens. This pursuit is the purpose of the following few pages.

The combination of Subject-Object theory and the Piagetian conception of stage-like growth brings together two influential streams of psychological discourse. On the one hand, Subject-Object Theory posits a conception of a person's relation to objects in his or her world, thereby providing the fundamental impetus for an understanding of the *construction* of a particular spiritual equilibrium. On the other hand, Piagetian formulations for growth supply a model of dynamic transformation into the spiritual system, thereby allowing a glimpse into how these Subject-Object constructions *develop* and evolve over time. As such, the two lines of discourse brought together by our investigation are those of constructivism and developmentalism.

According to Kegan's authoritative definitions, constructivism, in a nutshell, is the concept that a person actually selects, regulates, acts upon, makes decisions about, constitutes or *constructs* his or her apprehensions of reality (the natural result of the action of Subject-Object theory and meaning-making). Developmentalism is the notion that humanity evolves through qualitatively different eras of increasing complexity, according to regular principles of stability and change (the natural result of the action of the Piagetian concept of Assimilation-Accommodation-Decentration-Equilibrium).[46] Together, constructivism and developmentalism compose a framework of development in which currently held, identity-laden constructions of meaning-making are combined with the processes through which those very constructions change and grow over time. This is a wholistic and balanced combination of forces that is uniquely well-tailored to addressing the complexities of human growth as well as the abstractions of spirituality attenuation. As a result of this combination, constructivist-developmental theory is the basis of our approach to spiritual growth. I will now turn my attention to the concept of constructivism.

Constructivism removes us from the anti-Hegelian notion that we can observe reality in any objective sense. Rather, we literally put together,

---

46. Kegan, *In Over Our Heads*, 198; _____, *Evolving Self*, 8.

build, actively create the apprehensions we take from presenting internal and external stimuli. As such, recalling our discussion about the inextricability of the observer and the observed, constructivism states that it is the work of our consciousness that shapes and imparts coherence to our worldview. We are therefore active and mediating of our apprehensions of reality, whether or not we are consciously aware of our agency in this endeavor. Constructivism further implies that there is uniformity, stability, and endurance to our meaning-making—a sort of spiritual wholism that undergirds the entire process of understanding. As such, meaning construction is not undertaken in a moment-by-moment, construct-by-construct approach. Rather, the whole of spirituality is brought to bear on every instant of construction, acting as a background, a facilitator, an evaluator, and a guide.[47] Thus, it is not that a person constructs. It is rather that a person's complete constructed system, embedded in his or her level of spiritual evolution, further constructs newly found stimulus and experience (the hallmark of Assimilation). The level of evolution of our consciousness is what is referred to as our 'order of consciousness'. As such, our order of consciousness forms the constructed ground from which we view our experiences, from which we derive meaning from our experiences, and into which new experiences are assimilated and accommodated. Therefore, constructivism emphasizes the image of each person as the creator and perceiver of his or her own reality.

The power held within the process of construction and creation, however, has a double edge: understanding reality in a particular way requires, by its very definition, that we *not* understand it in another way. All aspects of meaning cannot find expression in a single act of apprehension. In other words, we engage in selective attention, an unwitting and discriminatory admission of part-narratives; being active in our seeing demands that we be blind to aspects we choose not to, or are simply unable to see.[48] Thus, for example, by choosing to interpret a particular act of gift-giving as a generous and joyful gesture, we choose not to perceive the same gesture as suspicious and dangerous. In light of this, a troubling question arises: having put our world together, are we aware of the fact that it is an invented reality, a made world? Are we critically aware of Absolute Spirit? Do we regularly look for some significantly different experience inside which a particular stimulus can still cohere? It

---

47. Kegan, *In Over our Heads*, 199.
48. Kegan, *In Over Our Heads*, 200; Kohlberg, *Moral Stages*; Fowler, *Stages of Faith*.

is my belief that we, more often than not, take our personal construction of reality as reality itself, and thereby close ourselves off to the impactful reciprocity we could foster with other Selves. We *make* sense, but we do not always own or take responsibility for that which we have made. We too easily leave out of our equations the agent of synthesis: our own order of consciousness.

A developmental perspective adds dynamism to our system of understanding. It provides the systemic impetus required to add movement, evolution, and emergence to an otherwise statically constructed system. In addition, it allows us to begin viewing the present moment as a passing occasion in the flow of time, utterly dependent on its past progress, and inextricably linked to its future trajectories. As such, a developmental perspective, approximating a Whiteheadian approach to perceiving time, renders every instant as nothing other than the next transient link on the ever-moving and never-breaking temporal chain.[49] As a corollary to this temporal pre-occupation, the developmental perspective applies itself to our current constructions of meaning-making, as they are framed by the panoply of meaning structures that have gone before us, and by which we are surrounded. Every phenomenon, then, gets looked at not only in terms of its placement in our unique lifecycle, but also in terms of its constructivist limits and strengths.[50] Therefore, meaning-making is seen as accomplished only through many years of continued practice, mediated by the consecutive constructions of our order of consciousness. These constructions form the basis of a personal sense of coherence (spirituality), and are thus interlinked as a pattern of succeeding evolutionary stages within consciousness. Thus, Emergence can only be achieved when a potential order of consciousness depends philosophically and mechanically, on the stage that preceded it.[51]

Development, then, is not simply the addition of new capabilities, but a continual process of the reorganization of consciousness in order to reach a more complex, more differentiated, and more integrated consciousness. The Self is not simply an agglomeration of traits and dispositions. Rather, it is the possessor of awareness, intentionality, recognition, continuity, and change, the congruence of the 'Me' and the 'I',

---

49. Whitehead, *Process and Reality*.

50. Kegan does an excellent job at dealing with these issues. Please see Kegan, *The Evolving Self*, 56.

51. Please see T. de Chardin, *The Phenomenon of Man*, 270.

all of which have been shaped and reshaped by the foibles of experience. This shaping and reshaping takes place through an ever-heightening pattern of stability and change (decentration). Like the idea of constructivism, then, developmentalism moves us beyond the traditionally static conceptions of human spirituality and consciousness, and takes us to a world of movement, progression, and dynamism. To quote Kegan,

> As constructivism directs us to the activity which underlies and generates the form of an order of consciousness, developmentalism directs us to the origins and processes by which the form came to be, and by which it will pass into a newer and more evolved form.[52]

In my opinion, this relationship is transformative, qualitative, and incorporative of the seemingly contradictory and elusive aspects of our spirituality. Thus, ontologically, we are dispositionally Emergent.

The complexity in our interrelation and growth as human beings lies in the fact that, although we reach levels of equilibrium that are relatively stable, we generally do not remain there forever. New experiences, stimuli, and information make themselves known and act as antithetical forces to our current constructions, thereby tipping our stability off-balance, and launching us into yet another round of transformative and emergent re-equilibration. As we have stated, this process of re-equilibration is most often experienced as difficult, painful, and unwelcome. As such, I have found that humanity tends to bind itself to unquestioned doctrines, narratives, and myths—harbingers of security, certainty, and personal control—that it once accepted through personal need and experience. We often fail to recognize that the truth we profess is often only *a* truth, one contiguous with our internal order of consciousness and with the general beliefs of the society in which we choose to live. I suggest that the path to successive stages of growth resides in the ability to see through the partial nature of these relative truths, lest we subject those around us to a dogma of which, unaware, we are stauch and convicted followers. Psychological problems, then, according to constructivist-developmentalism, are "not so much caused by rising up of the unconscious as by the deprivation of a full consciousness".[53] Full consciousness is not possible. It is the perfect alignment of all Objects

---

52. Kegan, *In Over Our Heads*, 31.
53. Jean Baker Miller in Kegan, *In Over Our Heads*, 198.

(true objectivity), integrated within a pure Subject (complete and integrated Selfhood), within a universal and cosmic order of consciousness. It is a state reserved only for the Divine 'I', a state that the struggling 'Me' will forever work to attain, knowing that there will forever be more to achieve. As such, the human spiritual struggle is not the refinement of a particular subjectivity, but rather the movement through subsequent stages of enhanced subjectivity, driven forward by the motivating and inspiring power of the Divine 'I'. Therefore, no human being has a full consciousness. We are all limited; we are all questing. Perpetually deprived of a fullness of consciousness, we construct spirituality only out of the meanings we have.

The most difficult and challenging experiences for us are those transformative moments in which we lose our subjectivity. These are the moments in which we feel out of control, unhinged, dispossessed, and impotent. These are the difficult times in which spiritual movement prohibits us from re-cognizing ourselves and our world, because whatever stimulus has arisen has trumped our Assimilative powers, has tipped our equilibrated state off-balance. Psychological pain, then, is the result of the inability to rise to the occasion and adapt, or of a more sinister and intentional resistance to the motion of growth. When our construction of reality becomes obsolete in the face of life's challenges, we experience great pain.

Psychologists, philosophers, and theologians often tell us that these personal crises can be interpreted as life-threatening dangers.[54] But life-threatening to whom? I believe that what is deeply threatened in these situations is the life and identity of the currently constructed Self-World equilibrium. In other words, a salient crisis can often sound the death toll to the old order of consciousness, to the old Self one knew oneself to be. It is in these moments that struggling individuals find that they cannot recognize their very selves, that they have somehow become strangers within their own skins. This is a common and well-known phenomenon. Kegan suggests that these moments are clearly identifiable as those in which a man feels 'beside himself', or a woman feels that there is a disjunction between what she witnesses herself doing, and who she knows herself to be.[55] This disjunction is the very symptom

---

54. Please see Roth, *Stages of Healing*, 23; Kegan, *The Evolving Self*, 266; Peck, *The Different Drum*, 199.

55. Kegan, *The Evolving Self*, 168.

of a larger process that has begun to take effect within spirituality. The process of Emergence itself.

As I have mentioned, Emergence is the spiritual act of breaking free of the merge, of differentiating from the fusion that was once considered synonymous with subjectivity. Throughout the process of Emergence, however, what is at stake is that very same notion of subjectivity. As such, as movement begins to take place within the spirituality of the transforming person, the security of that sense of self that is intrinsic to stable subjectivity is deeply shaken, thereby producing a crisis of identity recognition. It is for this reason that, in mid transformation, we often seem unrecognizable to ourselves—not because our consciousness is muddled with an arising stress, but rather because our very identity is shifting under our feet. As we weather the tensions of transformation, however (a process that can take very long indeed), we find a new plateau of equilibrium and inner peace. This new plateau is reached not by an old self having somehow dispelled a presenting crisis, but rather by a new and more integrated subjectivity that has emerged out of a redefinition of the Self-World equilibrium. Thus, healthy crisis navigation is literally the transformation of meaning, the very cost of evolution, and the objectification of old orders of consciousness. In reaction to the identity crisis introduced by this type of transformative event, transforming spiritualities are often besieged by experiences of frustration and recrimination, a storm of energy-laden affect that must precede the calm and stability of the new order of consciousness.

In these cases, I believe, the frustration is not so much a projection of insecurity onto the world at large, as it is a reactive experience of recognition and shame directed at the ineptitude and powerlessness felt in the situation. The recrimination is not so much a factor of resentment against something external, as it is a reaction of rebellion and distance from the internal equilibrium that is now perceived as inadequate. In simpler terms, these strong reactions serve to add emotional energy to the system, thereby attempting to ensure that any degree of backsliding into the old order of consciousness is strictly out of the question. Thus, internal personal defenses, which are very often characterized as relational and experiential dampers from which we ought to liberate ourselves, are, in this conception of growth, the guardians of personal stability, the promoters of internal intact-ness, and the concretization of adaptive responses. They are in fact the sentinels of assimilation, the agents which ensure that a system remains intact. Simultaneously, however, it is these defenses that act as the primary source of resistance against Accommodation, re-equilibration, and therefore, Emergence. It is in a person's self-protective marshalling of these defenses against the reorganization of meaning-making that Spiritual Leaders often experience the familiar reactions of increased social isolation, and even in some extreme cases, the appearance of self-protective delusions. So strong are these protective experiences and affective reactions that many feel ill-equipped to navigate their challenges alone.[56]

As such, throughout this process of re-equilibration and frustration, people often try to get counsel, in the hopes of returning to a calm spiritual plane, to a reconstruction of the world in which turmoil has ceased and in which both integration and differentiation have increased (the very heart of Emergence). As a consequence, the question we will further explore in the next section is self-evident: can teachers, counselors, ministers, and spiritual leaders walk with their clients, congregants, and students as they suffer through the stages of Emergence?

ESSENCE: NARRATIVE—THE SOUL OF CONSCIOUSNESS

Having taken a comprehensive view of the art and science of the evolution of consciousness as presented through the constructivist-developmental framework, there is only one task left to complete: a grounding of the various elements of the theory by an honest and probing appeal to the Pentateuchal narrative. It is the purpose of section to do this very thing.

I have already covered the tragic descent of human consciousness from the perfection of Eden to the fragmentation of Babel in chapter 2—the progressive regression of humanity's state into chaos, godlessness, and deep isolation. During this period of decline, the language of arrogance and self-sufficiency crept into the human vocabulary (Genesis 4:23–24), genealogies were provided to illustrate the diminishing life spans of Yahweh's people (Genesis 5), debauchery and distasteful behaviors ran rampant (Genesis 9:21), murder made its unwelcome appearance (Genesis 4:8), and the language of Creation was invoked and reversed to depict the successive steps Yahweh took in counteracting humanity's chosen downfall (Genesis 7:17–23). In short, the narrative

---

56. For more information on this, please see, Peck, *Different Drum;* Malone and Malone, *Windows of Experience;* Kegan, *In Over Our Heads;* Goleman, *Emotional Intelligence;* Goldberg, *Speaking with the Devil;* Capps, *Agents of Hope.*

outlines the state of un-integrated, unconnected, and irresponsible humanity—a state of whirlwinding decline. Most importantly, it also illustrates the paramount role played by human choice and responsibility in the progression of consciousness. As such, the role of human choice and responsibility will play as prominent a role in the reversal of this tragic decline—that is, the evolution of humanity's consciousness.

The story of this evolution begins with the appearance of Abram (Genesis 11:27). Abram, a lone and single man with no special powers to commend him, for reasons not mentioned in the narrative, decides to follow Yahweh (Genesis 12:4). Walter Moberly states that it was the infusion of this deliberate act of chosen innocence into the Pentateuchal narrative that changed the direction of history and the direction of the relationship between humanity and Yahweh.[57] It was this one man's decision to be committed to the counsel of the 'I' that began the process of redemption which was eventually to touch the whole of Creation. Therefore, it was neither a grand act of Holiness nor an inspired act of prophecy that caused Abram's actions to turn the course of history. It was nothing other than his committed choice—his choice to pursue Selfhood. For the rest of the Biblical text, Abram's faithful choice would be commended to him as one of the greatest dispositions of holy living.

Herein lies what I believe to be the first great lesson of humanity's evolution toward Holiness. The only requisite needed to halt the decline of consciousness, to change the course of personal development, and to invite the insights and guidance of the 'I' is nothing other than the simple and sincere decision to choose to align one's will toward the progression of Holiness. Just as Yahweh's promises of prosperity and relationship followed Abram from the point of their first meeting onward (Genesis 12), just as God's promise of direct guidance followed Moses from the Burning Bush onward (Exodus 4), just as the promise of God's protection followed Noah from the pledge onward (Genesis 6), so the promise of God's guidance and presence will endow the person who chooses growth and evolution from the first instant of choice onward. There is, however, a very personal responsibility attached to this choice. As an act of responsibility, evolution requires a decision to take ownership of the process of personal growth. As the movement of spirituality, evolution requires a decision to actually move. As such, according to the Pentateuchal theme, a person has only to decide that the progressing

---

57. Moberly, *The Old Testament*, 39.

aspects of spirituality (meaning and coherence) are his or her desired destiny, for the process of evolution to begin. Furthermore, so powerful is the act of choosing, that something as large as the redemption of an entire nation can rest on the decision of a single committed person to align his or her will to the guidance of the Divine 'I'.

For all of its complexity and pervasive ramifications, the constructivist-developmental theory can give scholars a powerful model for the elucidation of spiritual growth, but it can never present to the observant scholar any indication as to the impetus for the initial choice of the Subject to transform and Emerge. This personal act of choice is as much a scientific and artistic ambiguity as it is a spiritual mystery. What force causes one person to choose evolution and the other to choose stagnation? What motivation prompts one person to align his or her will to the guidance and encouragement of the Divine 'I' and another person to wallow in idle entitlement? The question of a person's election of Yahweh is as mysterious to me as the question of Yahweh's election of Israel. It is a mystery that has baffled scholars and philosophers for millennia, and as such, is as much a mystery to the current state of the constructivist-developmental theory as it ever was to theologians of old. One of the areas of further development of this line of study is to conduct detailed research from a constructivist-developmental viewpoint in order to shed whatever light can be gleaned on this ephemeral and ultimately graceful topic. What we can continue discussing with some confidence, however, is the further progression of the Pentateuchal narrative as it illuminates the constructivist-developmental conception of spiritual growth. So, on with the story of Abram.

Immediately on the heels of the first communication, Yahweh promises Abram a new land (Genesis 12:1). Unlike other characters in the Primeval cycle, however, Abram will not stumble upon this land as a wandering stranger (like Cain), nor will he settle in this new land as a result of a forced exile (like the builders of the Tower of Babel). Rather, Abram will enter the new land by way of Yahweh's explicit guidance and direction. This promise will extend its influence right up to the very end of the Pentateuchal narrative. Yahweh, as a physical incarnation of the Pillar of Fire or Pillar of Cloud, actively leads the people of Israel through the desert, toward the destination he has promised. Consequently, the arrival at this land of promise becomes not only a goal for the descendants of Abram, but also its very destiny, its mission as ordained by

Yahweh Himself. Furthermore, the quest toward this new land is held within a matrix of powerful promises made to Israel by Yahweh: the promises of relationship with Yahweh, uncountable descendants, and commanding Divine blessing (Genesis 12:2–3). So powerful are these promises that they reappear continuously throughout the Pentateuchal cycle and affirm the expected destiny of a relationship with Yahweh to Abram's descendants, even when those descendants choose to behave in unseemly and deceitful manners (Genesis 28:13, 33:30, 35:11, 46:3, Exodus 3:5, 3:15, 6:2). As such, from the moment the promise of land is first uttered, a simple geographical location becomes fraught with divine purpose and promise. Moberly states that this promise of a new land symbolizes not just a home, but also a new type of community.[58] Unlike the human creation of the city of Babel, this new land will be created and guided by Yahweh Himself, and the inhabitants that will reside there will be the people of God. In addition, the appearance of a commanding blessing is of particular importance at this point in the narrative. Just as the world began with a divine blessing, so does the progressive creation of this new world begin with a divine blessing. By the end of the Primeval Cycle, curse had dominated the tale. Now, with the simple act of renewal provided by the choice of Abram to follow Yahweh, God's grace reintroduces the beauty and comfort of blessing into the world.

We have arrived at a second lesson of the Pentateuchal narrative. This Promised Land, this anticipated community of God promised to Israel, is now the destination to which the 'Me' must strive. As stated in chapter 2, the Hebrew belief was that descendants bore not only the namesake and reputation of their ancestors, but also their mission, their allegiances, and their dispositions. Consequently, the destination of the entire Judeo-Christian culture, as descendants of Abraham, is the very Promised Land mentioned in Genesis chapter 12. Thus, the Holiness of the people of God, which is embodied in and represented by their arrival at the Promised Land, will be achieved through the promised relationship of Yahweh with Israel. From His position at the center of the people (the 'Me'), Yahweh leads a less-than-appreciative Israel to the land first promised to Abram. Hence, it is my belief that the Promised Land is reached through a devoted pursuit of Selfhood.

Selfhood is a state of congruence and presence. As we have already seen, it is a state of deep relationship between the 'I' and the 'Me', where

---

58. Moberly, *The Old Testament*, 28.

neither party confounds its identity with that of the other. As such, it creates a spiritual space of clarity, insight, and direction. Because of its insight and direction, it undergirds and promotes the development of meaning and coherence constructed by the Self. Consequently, Selfhood forges connections between the past and the future of spirituality, projecting its willful and informed preferences into the further development of the Self—which matures through cycles of autonomy and integration. Thus, Selfhood is not only a state of congruence and presence— it is also a state of responsible connection between the 'I' and 'Me', a connection which telescopes its rewards into the further development and evolution of the Self and its actions. Consequently, true Selfhood is a state of surrender and reciprocity between the various elements of Self. It is therefore the destiny of spiritual growth, and results in further promoting the connection between the 'I' and 'Me', in furthering the capability of the Self to produce congruent works, and in furthering the Self's commitment to spiritual prosperity and evolution. This conception of evolution is attested to in the Pentateuchal narrative. The Promised Land, the convergence of the wills of the 'I' and the 'Me' of the narrative, is a place of divine purpose and promise. It is the seat of abundance and nurturance (Exodus 3:17). And, most importantly, it is home. As part of the Judeo-Christian heritage, this aspiration to find our spiritual home—our Selves—falls to every person who has made the choice to pursue Selfhood and Holiness. In addition, the quest to this home comes held within a matrix of powerful promises: the promise of relationship (further connection between 'I' and 'Me'), the promise of descendants (further ability to create congruent works), and the promise of blessing (further impetus to pursue spiritual evolution). As such, the evolution of Self is not a haphazard and random series of events. Rather, the Pentateuchal narrative teaches that it is a directional and purposeful drive toward a land of peace—a home—promised by the guidance of the 'I'. In this way, the definition of Holiness as the drive to spirituality focused on the Divine is supported and further informed by the image of the Divinely guided quest for the Promised Land.

This guidance of the 'I' toward the Promised Land, however, was not presented to Abram only once. The Pentateuchal narrative describes a second meeting between Abram and Yahweh in which the promises are restated and renewed (Genesis 15). In this episode however, Yahweh actively adds a very important element to the promises. For the first time since their first encounter, Yahweh requires something on the part of Abram—the commitment to pursue Holiness. Whereas the first set of promises was given freely by grace, the restatement of the promises requires Abram to cooperate and to actually change his behavior to reflect the directives of Yahweh. As such, what was once the choice of Abram (to follow the Divine 'I') has now become the fundamental mission of Abraham (to purposely seek out and obey the Divine 'I'). The same charge is not reserved for Abram alone, of course. It is repeated throughout the Biblical narrative to all the descendants of the Patriarchal line: Isaac hears the charge before meeting Abimelech (Genesis 26:5), Jacob dreams of Yahweh's presence (Genesis 28:10–15), Moses hears Yahweh's intentions for Israel (Exodus 3:15), Yahweh charges Israel with this responsibility with a direct command (Leviticus 11:45). The placement of the charge to Holiness in the narrative is also indicative of its primacy within Yahweh's scheme. In each of the cases mentioned above, the directive to Holiness served as the first point of dialogue between Yahweh and the members of the 'Me'. It was therefore, the very ground upon which and the fundamental meaning within which the further relationship between the parties was to progress.

Herein lies the third lesson of the Pentateuchal narrative. Whereas we may find ourselves qualitatively transformed by the simple choice of turning our consciousness to the evolution of spirituality, and whereas the promise held within this choice is nothing less than the attainment of a spiritual home abounding in nurturance, this transformation only goes so far. Thereafter, the Biblical narrative teaches that purposeful action must accompany the pure hearted choice. Therefore, in order to promote human evolution, the alignment of the will to the progression of consciousness must be accompanied by the execution of that will in the integration of growth. The 'Me' listens to the 'I' and the 'Me' *acts* in accordance with the guidance of the 'I'. And, as a result, the Self emerges and evolves. As the charge to Holiness challenges every member of the people of God to assimilate challenges, surrender to the Divine 'I', and accommodate solutions in order to produce new and more congruent relationships with all of Creation, so the story of constructivist-developmentalism outlines the progression of the Self as taking place through the Piagetian framework of Assimilation–Accommodation–Decentration–Re-equilibration. According to this psychological scheme, it is not enough to simply decide that personal growth is a worthy goal.

Through the juxtaposition of Thesis and Antithesis, Piaget described the Emergence of a new Subjectivity, a renewed equilibrium of the Self that was the result of Synthesis. This act of growth and evolution is not an automatic by-product of the choice to cherish personal development. Rather, it is the result of a willful act of effort, focusing energy on the complexities of the challenge at hand, and laboring tirelessly to come to a new plateau of centeredness (Decentration). Selfhood, then, is not achieved through an anonymous and effortless system of personal change. It is achieved through an effortful alignment of one's personal will to pursue spirituality and Holiness through deliberate and cogent acts, which are consistent with Selfhood development. Consequently, when the 'Me' is charged with the activity of Holiness, it is being directed to be zealous in the development of its Self. The choice to want Selfhood (spirituality), must be coupled with the action of pursuing Selfhood (Piagetian scheme of development), in order for the great destiny of the Promised Land to come to fruition (autonomy, integration, responsibility, connectedness, Holiness).

The story of Abraham and the Promised Land does not end here, however. In fact, it is just beginning. The first obstacle to the fulfillment of this evolution of community is expressed shortly after the ratification of the agreement between Yahweh and Abraham. The Promised Land, the land of Canaan, is already inhabited by another people. Consequently, the claiming of this Promised Land would involve a process that is significantly more complicated than a simple appearance on the scene and a staking of a claim. Rather, the claiming of this Promised Land would clearly involve struggle, difficulty, and even war. Throughout the entire Pentateuchal narrative, the motif of struggle and opposition pervades every episode: Abraham traveling as an alien through the Land (Genesis 20–22), Jacob and Esau clash from the moment of conception (Genesis 25), Isaac being deceived by Jacob (Genesis 27), Jacob wrestling with the Angel (Genesis 32), Joseph imprisoned (Genesis 40), Israel enslaved by Egypt (Exodus 1), Moses' birth (Exodus 2), Pharaoh's disposition toward Israel (Exodus 5), grumbling and rebellion among the people of Israel (Numbers 11), and the many wars waged by Israel to conquer Canaan. To me, these ominous episodes provide the fourth lesson supplied by the Pentateuchal narrative for spiritual growth.

This lesson can be simply stated: the attainment of Holiness is not a resistance-free activity. It is not simply a choice that is followed by an automatic transformation of will. It is not an entitlement of the 'Me' nor is it the wide and easy road. It is in fact the road less traveled, the road of effort, the road of work. It is as much the road to fulfillment and evolution as it is the road to loss and pain. Please recall that constructivist-developmental theory draws one of its main tenets from Subject-Object theory. This element of constructivist-developmentalism is greatly analogous to the concept of this painful 'road less traveled'. It states that in order to achieve greater levels of autonomy and integration, that which was once part of the Subject must be re-cognized as an Object and integrated into the new subjectivity. In essence, this process applies to all aspects of human life, even to identity itself. In fact, one of the most painful, and yet one of the most growthful events in the evolution proposed by constructivist-developmental theory is this very activity of reshaping and redefining identity to better cope with the arising complexities (oppositions) of life. The Pentateuchal narrative reflects this fact by stating that the Promised Land of union with God lies after a lengthy and uncertain campaign of conquest. Similarly, a Subject must be confronted by opposing forces, be thwarted in its well-traveled tracks, and be forced to wage a virtual war against its own neurotic proclivities in order to extract from itself an element that will, from that moment forward, be seen as a new Object. This is the very process described above as Emergence. It is through this process of Emergence that the 'Me' evolves and approaches the Promised Land of Holiness.

The creation of this new Object, however, carries with it a steep price. The emergence of a new Subject comes only after the sacrifice of the old Subjectivity. It is no surprise, then, that the theme of sacrifice figures prominently in the Pentateuchal narrative. From the moment of the expulsion from the Garden, the practice of sacrifice was a mediating and prominent force in the relationship of Yahweh with His people. It was presented as a regular activity of daily life (Cain and Abel), a ritual of thanks (Noah), a medium of obedience and faith (Abraham), a requisition for guidance (Isaac), a strengthening of relationship (Moses), and, most importantly, as an act of atonement (Moses and Israel). As such, it evolved as the primary means of signaling the desire to devote oneself to the guidance and purview of the great 'I'. Consequently, sacrifice exemplified an act of completeness (in relationship, intent, and action), and was the sole means of reconciliation between the people of Israel and Yahweh. Yahweh's pledge to never repeat the devastation of the Flood was accompanied by an act of sacrifice, Abraham's evolution of consciousness which resulted from the sparing of Isaac was accompanied by an act of sacrifice, the termination of Jacob's lengthy pilgrimage back to Bethel was accompanied by an act sacrifice, the liberation of the Israelite people on the banks of the Red Sea was accompanied by an act of sacrifice, and acts of impurity and uncleanness were washed away by sacrifice. Hence, the theme of sacrifice couples itself with some very important concepts—life, transformation, pilgrimage, liberation, and atonement. Mann goes so far as to state that within the Pentateuchal narrative, the sacrificial ritual is the only means provided to Israel through which to reconcile to Yahweh.[59] It is both a formal and a repeatable resource of reconciliation. Consequently, I believe that it is a practice that is provided for by Yahweh Himself.

Similarly, in the constructivist-developmental framework of spiritual growth, transformation of consciousness carries with it the promise of renewed vitality. This transformation, however, only arises from the 'death', the sacrifice, of an old way of being. It is only through sacrificing the old that the new Subjectivity has occasion to Emerge. Therefore, in accordance with the images of the Pentateuchal narrative, sacrifice of the old Subjectivity brings about the new life of transformation by allowing the emerging consciousness to take shape and thrive; sacrifice of the old Subjectivity is the result of a long pilgrimage to a new and greater state of personal awareness; sacrifice of the old Subjectivity is a liberation from outdated, impractical, and destructive habits and beliefs; and, most importantly, sacrifice of the old Subjectivity is the primary and prerequisite event through which the new Subjectivity can reunite and relate to Yahweh. This reunification of the more aware, more mature, and more connected Self with the 'I' of Yahweh is, to my mind, the very epitome of the concept of atonement.

The consequence of atonement is clearly delineated in the Pentateuchal narrative. After the sacrificial ritual, life does not continue as usual—there is always a change. Subtle though it might be, from the appearance of Abraham onward, the practice of sacrifice resulted in a transformation of the consciousness of the character worshipping Yahweh. Abraham exhibits greater freedom in his relationship to Yahweh after the sparing of Isaac;[60] the Jacob who pours oil on the altar at Bethel

---

59. Mann, *The Book of Torah*, 121.
60. Please see Knight, *Theology as Narrative*, 56.

is wiser and more surrendered to Yahweh's will, than the Jacob who was the deceiver of the earlier chapters of Genesis;[61] after their sacrifice, the people of Israel walk away from the banks of the Red Sea no longer a slave nation—for the first time in centuries. The consciousness that develops after the act of sacrifice is at once a more autonomous, differentiated, and confident as well as a more integrated, wise, and connected consciousness than that which preceded the sacred act. As such, it is the very movement of spirituality—evolution—that is made manifest by these episodes.

Consequently, I believe that it is God's will that we evolve and grow to greater levels of autonomy and connectedness. I believe that the guidance of the Divine 'I' consistently leads the committed 'Me' to higher levels of Holiness. Transformation, then, is a Holy pursuit and is the very inheritance of the Judeo-Christian tradition. It is, in my opinion, the very mission of the 'Me' that seeks to relate to and know a world full of meaning, and coherence. Stagnation (as exemplified by Lamech, Lot, and Laban) does not lead to triumph, wisdom, or success. Rather, as in the examples of these unfortunate characters, stagnation leads to obsolescence, loss, and despair. Therefore, the attainment of Selfhood, the committed discipleship to the Divine 'I', the willingness to be faithfully led, and the openness to the daunting act of sacrifice all contribute to the Emergence of a new Israel, a complete Self, and transformed consciousness—in short, an evolved Subjectivity. Thus, I have outlined how the constructivist-developmental constructs of Spirituality, Evolution, Assimilation, Accommodation, Re-equilibration, Decentration, Emergence, and Selfhood are all attested to, furthered, and deepened by the Pentateuchal narrative. It is not Yahweh's will that we follow Him blindly through the desert of life. Rather, it is His revealed intention that we choose a relationship with Him, and through it, transform our spirits into Selves, which are capable of more clearly seeing.

A FINAL THOUGHT

In my estimation, a spiritually intelligent life offers us a series of redemptions and mini-resurrections; an evolution with the promise of further challenges to arise later. The triumph of discovering a new part of the Self brings with it the promise of finding further fragments of the Self to-

---

61. Please see Alexander, *From Paradise to the Promised Land*, 145.

morrow. Within this insight lies the kernel of peace. After all, if development and evolution are equated with the event of being human, then the comfort of healing is our Divine destiny, and the challenges we face are the very movements of the *Logos* in our *Psyche*. In an age when psychology is becoming nothing short of a secular religion, Spiritual Leaders must humbly and diligently, equip themselves with powerful tools that will foster and promote spiritual growth and awareness in the Selves of each of their clients, as well as in their own Selves. It is the purpose of the next section to provide spiritual leaders with a framework, steeped in Natural Theology, grounded in Science, and enveloped in empathy and compassion. Should they choose to accept it, I believe that the attitudes stipulated in the constructivist-developmental approach to spiritual growth will allow the Holy teachings of the Bible to address the very meaning-making and makeup of consciousness within which clients are embedded. To my mind, this is the epitome of bringing God into the deepest ground of the Self.

SECTION TWO

Seeing: Thought and Action in Spiritual Leadership

Prologue Revisited

We have discussed the constructivist-developmental framework by which spiritual growth occurs. It is a framework of gradual and qualitative evolution that progresses through the mechanism of the decentration and transformation of the Subject-Object balance of the individual. A change in our personal order of consciousness is not simply a change in the figures and forms of our attention. Rather, it is a fundamental change in the very ground from which we attend. Although the knowledge of this framework provides a powerful tool in self-awareness, it is the purpose of applying this scheme to the Spiritual Leadership relationship that is the focus of this book. As such, the constructivist-developmental Spiritual Leader's effort to provide good and nurturing company for his or her client's journey through evolving orders of meaning-making, is based on the keen understanding of the inner experience of a process that, for the client, is often interpreted as a threat to one's very identity.

In the Prologue to Section 1, I stated the two main arguments set out by this work. The first is that the process of human evolution takes place through a process of emergence of ever-increasing forms of complexity within a developing person's equilibrium; the second is my belief that Spiritual Leaders are called to humbly and prayerfully accompany clients through this process of Emergence by co-constructing with the client a therapeutic culture of embeddedness. This therapeutic culture of embeddedness involves goal orientation, environment-creation, attitudinal alignment, and practical techniques. Spiritual Leaders achieve this delicate end by committing unwaveringly to the personal evolution of the client. An unwavering commitment to the person of the client implies a practiced ability to walk with the client through difficult transitions, and an ability to be a balanced witness to the sacred process of the client's spiritual evolution. It is now time to turn our attention to the second of these arguments. In its distilled essence, it is an argument meant to address the conduct and purpose of Spiritual Leaders.

Beholding a client's evolution is a sacred experience—a witnessing of the activity of a person struggling with spirituality. This process is an activity of humanity that transcends culture, environment, and life phase. As such, spiritual growth is the fundamental and universal inheritance of the entire human race. According to Kegan, such a personal activity has as much to do with the "adult's struggle to recognize himself or herself, as it has to do with a young child's struggling to recognize his or her true boundaries; it has as much to do with the teenager's delicate balance of loyalty to personal satisfaction and loyalty to the preservation of reciprocal relationships, as it has to do with a baby's effort to finally balance on two legs."[1] Seen in this light, the activity of spiritual growth is confirmed as the fundamental activity of humanity at all levels of its development.

The ability of Spiritual Leaders to better perceive this sacred process increases their recruitability to the welfare of the person confronting them. I define recruitability as a person's openness to the intimate attending of another.[2] It is the compassionate and visionary embracing and the whole-hearted willingness to be dispatched to the aid of an Other. As such, the greater my recruitability, the greater my ability to truly see the struggles and needs of my care seekers and clients—the greater my ability to provide a truly transformation-oriented, Emergence-promoting, and nourishing Other that can walk with them in their loneliness, contradict them in their stability, and be present with them throughout the strains of growth. The process of being drawn into the experience of an Other and attending to them as they struggle to re-equilibrate their structure of spirituality is, in its very essence, the process of better seeing the careworn person before us. Thus, we become a witness to their developing identities. Therefore, the need to be seen and recognized may change in its complexity; but, it will never change in its primacy and intensity.

Throughout the process of this complexity, spiritual development occurs within the client's individual and personal spiritual understanding; it is therefore this understanding which needs to be transformed. It is the client who is the agent of this transformation. Consequently, I

---

1. Kegan, *The Evolving Self*, 15.

2. For more on recruitability and attending, please see Bellous, *Educating Faith*, 70–76.

believe that it is not indoctrination that we need, although our present supply of it is tragically plentiful. Rather, what we need to provide our clients is stimulation: dialogue, debate, nurturance, contradiction, all of which take place in a structure that gives each client the opportunity to grow, evolve, and uncover ways in which to more adequately and constructively make meaning. As such, I reject the varied and pervasive attempts at rationalization, which exonerate Spiritual Leaders from the great challenge of this empathic and fundamentally loving method of help. I believe that the introduction of a diligent and meticulous Spiritual Leader into the life of a person can be one of the single greatest factors of influence on that person's meaning-making and spiritual development. This life-developing connection is exceptionally based on the Spiritual Leader's ability and availability to be recruited to the help of the person. For Spiritual Leaders, this process is so personally vested, arduous, and intimate that it threatens to bring them face-to-face with the challenging vagaries of life. It is in this confrontation that the risks and challenges of Spiritual Leadership become highlighted against the backdrop of a caring relationship. However much we learn about the process of being of help, it is my belief that we should never protect and shield ourselves from these risks and challenges. It is these risks that separate true help from advice-giving, consolation, and, worse yet, reassurance. It is in running and preserving these risks to truly care that we preserve and protect the connection between us. It is in respecting and allowing the evolution in spirit of all those around us that we enhance the life we share, and bring into greater existence the Kingdom of God.

The base argument for this section states that the Spiritual Leader is responsible for co-creating a culture of embeddedness that involves goal orientation, environment-creation, attitudinal alignment, and practical techniques. The next several chapters will take each of these topics and apply them to the Spiritual Leadership relationship.

4

The Goals of Spiritual Leadership

THE HEART OF THE constructivist-developmental framework is not an elucidation of elegant philosophical and scientific tenets of development; nor is it the determination of intertwined and interacting mechanics of re-equilibration. Rather, its very impetus lies in its ability to provide a vocabulary and conceptual basis through which we can view the processes of meaning-making, evolution, decentration, subject-object re-balancing, and Emergence—the very building blocks of Self-development and spiritual growth. Accordingly, it is to this process and its experiences that I believe Spiritual Leaders should focus their energies so that they will not fall into the ever-present trap of focusing on the things a client *cannot* do, or worse yet, on things they, as therapists, insist on doing for their own self-concepts, system defense, and meaning edification. Instead, I believe that Spiritual Leaders may come to a greater understanding and a vocal validation of the sacred path that has led the client to the present state of maturity and achievement. As such, I believe that Spiritual Leadership helps clients in a particular way. Although a comparison of the various approaches to Spiritual Leadership is beyond the scope of these pages, the focus of this section is to elucidate the details and mechanisms of this 'particular way' of approaching Spiritual Leadership.

One of the greatest consequences of this understanding and validation is a replacement of the concept of simple truth (the supposedly correct representation of states or events in an external world), by the notion of viability.[1] To the biologist, a living organism is viable so long as it manages to survive in its environment. To the constructivist-developmentalist, a state of consciousness is viable so long as it proves adequate in the context of current meaning-making, so long as its Assimilative faculties remain cogent. In other words, in the constructivist-devel-

---

1. For more, please see Steffe and Gale, *Constructivism in Education*, 7.

opmental framework, a construction of meaning-making is viable so long as its equilibrium of Subject and Object is sufficiently evolved to effectively weather the complexities presented to consciousness. No sooner do irreconcilable complexities (antitheses) arise than the current equilibrium is rendered unviable and in great need of transformation. It is to this process of meaning-making and to the challenged viability of troubled clients that Spiritual Leaders turn their attention. The goal of Spiritual Leadership, then, is four-fold: first, Spiritual Leaders are to engage in a disciplined development of non-arbitrary perceptual standards that protect and nurture the opportunities that arise for the evolution of the client's personal consciousness—a consciousness which the client no longer deems to be viable; second, Spiritual Leaders are to nurture their clients into a mindset of self-determination; third, Spiritual Leaders are to enter their clients' worlds by engaging in sensitive and respectful investigations of clients' Historical Space; and fourth, Spiritual Leaders are to cultivate insight within the spiritual systems of their clients, and use this insight to add energy to the transformative event. The purpose of this chapter is to explore these four goals of Spiritual Leadership.

1. UNDERSTANDING HISTORICAL SPACE

It is no secret that the Spiritual Leadership relationship is not limited to the scope of the present moment. Clients come to Leaders as both works in progress and completed packages of history and experience. As a result, one of the main challenges of evolution within the therapeutic relationship is the conquering of the patterns of the past that hold many drives and preferences captive, often outside of the client's conscious awareness. As such, Spiritual Leaders are confronted by a vast and interlocked network of meaning-making matrices that affect the therapeutic relationship. In the following paragraphs, I will discuss this historical aspect of the client's presentation.

As I have mentioned, constructivist-developmentalism is a humanistic and psychodynamically influenced theory. As such, it carries within it a strong interest in the experiences that led a client to make himself or herself present for a consultation. It is the effect of the combined forces that have sway in one's environment that I refer to when I speak of Historical Space.

I define Historical Space as the matrix of forces that are concretized in the current subjectivity of any single person. Whiteheadian process philosophy has much to inform my notion of Historical Space. According to Whitehead, all actual entities in the universe are not so much physical presences as they are the concrescence of the extraordinary array of forces that find a common synergy. As such, he stipulates that the driving force of actual-ness in the universe is affect—where the affect from all possible sources combine in particular arrays of coordination in order to bring an actual entity into being. In other words, entities only exist because of their relations (affections) to other entities.

To use an example: imagine that there is a jewel hanging in space—a beautiful, shining ruby, expertly polished and wondrously large. Imagine also that this ruby has an infinite number of polished faces on it. Now, around that ruby, add the image of another four jewels, each of them boasting an infinite number of faces. Imagine further that every one of the infinite facets of each of the five jewels forms a bright reflection in each of the facets of each of the other jewels. The interrelations between these five jewels is thus staggering. As a final stroke in the refinement of our image, increase the number of jewel to an infinite amount, each of them having facets that reflect the infinite facets from every other jewel in the array. What we are left with, if we pursue this image to its logical conclusion is a dizzying matrix of interrelations, where every entity is somehow related to every other entity. And now, the final master stroke. Until this instant, our image has been based on the prior existence of entities that find a reflection in one another's surfaces. Let us now reverse this relationship: let us suppose for our image that any one of the jewels can only exist if it finds itself reflected in the other jewels. In other words, the relationship introduced by the reflections is determinative of that jewels existence. As such, there will no longer be the possibility of a jewel devoid of relation (since that jewel would no longer exist). All we are left with is the power of relationship, and the concrescence of those relationships in the bodies of the jewels.

Whitehead's conception of entities is analogous to this complex and staggering image. All entities exist because they are the concrescence of determinative and affective relationships. Thus, the ontology of the universe is utterly complex, relational, and interlocked. It is to this conception of integration that I appeal when I refer to the concept of Historical Space.

I think of Historical Space as the concrescence of the forces of a person's entire past and present circumstances. As such, just as the jewels had infinite interrelations with one another, I believe that the various and sundry elements of Historical Space find existence in their interrelation. As such, each is a primary driver of concrescence while simultaneously being utterly dependent on its relations to the other elements. Historical Space, then, is an intricately woven fabric of forces that shape spirituality. It is my belief that these forces can be categorized in three dimensions: Context, Individuality, and Requisite.

a. Context: The Dimension of Depth

It should not come as a surprise that the first element of Historical Space is the formal aspect of the temporal surround inside which a person finds himself or herself. This Dimension encompasses the totality of the matrix of past and present circumstances that are effectual upon a particular subjectivity. Context is the sum total of the background of any one person, the accretion of ancestral material, and the fundamental inheritance of the order of consciousness, as well as the extra-subjective complexities of current living that are determinative of and influential upon subjectivity. As such, Context is a deep and penetrating element in Historical Space that provides the basic narratives within which spirituality will anchor itself. Context provides the first principles of situational placement and effect, the ground from which spirituality's circumstances are developed, and a determinative force, shaping the quality of spirituality's possibilities. Context is that extra-subjective aspect of Selfhood that works upon us, and that we cannot be effectual on in return (the very definition of first principles).[2] It is the inescapable milieu that embeds us, the ubiquitous position that is definitive of us, and the intricate matrix that interweaves with us. In short, it is the container that holds spirituality. Because of this all-encompassing complexity, I have come to

---

2. In our discussion of Subject-Object Theory, we defined Subject as that on which we cannot be effectual. In that context, we were referring to one's fundamental self-identity within the matrix of a world of objects. In the case of the Dimension of Context, our inability to be effectual upon it is slightly more complex. In the case of phases and stages (discussed as part of the component of individuality), we are able, with much introspection and compassionate guidance, to achieve a level of objectivity. In the case of history and culture, however, the influences presented to subjectivity are not accessible to the executive force of subjectivity because of their temporal and ontological distance. The best that can be achieved in these situations, is a fundamental re-definition in how we choose to 'mean' these aspects. It is for this reason that I believe that the Dimension of Context provides the first principles of Historical Space, the ground of subjectivity's context.

think of the Dimension of Context as made up of three seminal components: history, condition, and culture. I will turn my attention to each of these components in turn.

I define history as the experiential and mythological narrative, spanning bygone periods, that provides the fundamental impetus for determining a person's placement in the flow of time, progress, and evolution. This narrative informs spirituality of one's ancestral achievements as well as one's heritage and its proclivities. It informs spirituality of the conventions of the family of origin and of the possibilities and dreams espoused by the familial culture. It also provides personal mythology to consciousness—internalized and deeply held stories about power, success, failure, struggle, triumph, experience, betrayal, aggrandizement, arrogance, humility, and possibility. These narratives, from the deepest understandings of familial preferences to the remotest expanses of ancestral victory, provide the semiological ground, the founding substrate, from which meaning-making will find direction. They are the very course of extra-personal movement in which conceptions of Self and Other will be planted. These narratives are therefore the anchors of the meaning system, providing profundity and weight to an otherwise individualized construction. Their influence on subsequent meaning-making is profound, although often unattended to and taken for granted. In fact, these narratives are some of the most exigent elements of Self, possessing a commanding hold on consciousness and meaning construction, and therefore require frequent and repeated rounds of objectification (if their effects are to be perceived, understood, and used in fostering the health of spirituality). As such, the component of history is the fullness of one's personal back story as it comes to act decisively on meaning-making, and thus, spirituality. It is the determinant of temporal movement and direction, and therefore of subjectivity's basic placement within that movement. It provides a central ideal of the contextual Self. Therefore, in response to this central idea, spirituality will simultaneously be engaged in two fundamental and counterbalancing activities: the fight for the preservation of history's dearly held values and meaning; and the struggle for the achievement of personal objectivity and freedom from history's grasp. The component of history, then, is the sum total of my lived experiences, my espoused myths, and my founding contexts. It is the very ground out of which subjectivity will interpret direction, aberration, and need, and therefore is a fundamental concern of the Spiritual Leadership interaction.³ And yet, explorations of history must take place within a current environment if they are to have life within a client's current subjectivity. It is my belief that this current-state embeddedness is mediated through 'condition', the second component in the Dimension of Context.

By condition, I am referring to one's unique placement within the current reality of the psychosocial matrix. As such, I turn my attention to the unique aspects of phase negotiation and stage incarnation within each subjectivity. According to Karen Eriksen, a phase is a psychosocial construction which refers to an interval of time in the lifespan of a person during which certain themes, such as autonomy, trust, career development, or family formation, are ascendant.⁴ Seminal work on phase progression was conducted by Erik Erickson, and resulted in an incisive and staggeringly useful explication of the needs of the various life phases.⁵ According to Erik Erickson, our life contexts and age together form a nexus of influence through which we toil to vanquish the unique struggles of our particular, age-appropriate phase. As an example, infants, in reaction to the positive and negative proclivities of the caretaking environment, develop (or fail to develop) a sense of fundamental trust in the world. Trust development is the phase-appropriate challenge *par excellence* of infancy, and is also the very ground from which the next psychosocial phase-development can take place. As such, according to Erikson, each era of life, from infancy into old age, has its corresponding phase challenge, and these challenges critically affect how meaning is made, how direction is chosen, and how social integration and success is conceived. Thus, a phase is the psychosocial exigency of age and is therefore externally imposed on the subjectivity. In addition, successful and constructive phase negotiation forms the foundation for future phase-oriented challenges. In other words, according to Erikson, phase maturity is only achieved through a cumulative accretion of prior-phase mastery. For example, a child that does not succeed in developing a degree of constructive trust in the seminal years of infancy will not be able to develop 'will', the next phase challenge (in later childhood). Consequently, phase determinations will help guide both clients and

---

3. Some strategies for the elucidation of history in a constructivist-developmental framework are provided in Chapter 7.

4. Eriksen, "Constructivist and Developmental Identity".

5. Erickson, *Childhood and Society*, 264.

Spiritual Leaders toward experiences, challenges, and subjective blocks that may need resolution, if Emergence is to be constructively fostered. Whereas phase is an externally imposed construct determined by cultural proclivities and age, a stage is a internal construct affecting orders of consciousness and the nature and direction of meaning-making.

A stage can be defined as the unique meaning-making alignment, based on one's subject-object balance, that is determinative of one's order of consciousness. As such, stages give an indication of the underlying orientation to the world that a person holds in consciousness. Stages are defined by subjective identity and by the protection of that identity in the face of countervailing stimuli. As such, a stage is a subject-object equilibrium that has executive and effective assimilative powers in the face of life's challenges and experiences. It is the very construct that must undergo decentration, should spiritual evolution take place. Stage movement is the very basis of subject–object theory and a main object of the constructivist-developmental framework of growth. In addition, although stages are usually linked with age-based development, such correlations are simply convenient conventions of categorizations. A person need not progress through stage incarnations with the passing of age. As such, to develop an understanding of a person's stage, as well as the unique incarnation that stage has taken within him or her, is crucial to a holistic apprehension of the presenting care-seeker.[6] Such apprehensions guide Spiritual Leader's in effectively understanding their clients' meaning directions, joining their clients in those meanings, and are the underlying drivers of truly client-centered therapeutic practices. As such, stage determination and a responsible application of that knowledge are fundamental tools in the constructivist-developmental Spiritual Leader's repertoire, and are perceptual lenses through which Leaders can come to better understand the phenotypes of clients' subjectivities, as well the effect of current culture on those phenotypes. It is to the effect of culture, the third component of the Dimension of Context, that I turn my attention next.

By culture, I refer to the specific and local communal biases that surround and infuse subjectivity. As such, every person is embedded in a concentric array of cultures, from the culture of the family of ori-

---

6. It is beyond the scope of this work to elucidate stage theory. For more information, please see Fowler, *Stages of Faith;* Kegan, *Evolving Self;* Kohlberg, *Moral Stages;* Erikson, *Childhood and Society;* Piaget, *Constructions of Reality;* Perry, *College Years.*

gin, to the culture of the chosen society; from the shaded preferences of the generalized global mindset to the specific biases of a community of practice. In almost all cases, these cultures interlink to provide consciousness with a system of value, ethics, morality, art, expression, and communal signification that is difficult to distill. Unlike the component of 'history' that outlined one's back story, culture refers to one's current and diverse milieu. Unlike 'condition' that refers to one's place on life's timeline, culture refers to environmental influences that exert their effect on subjectivity in real time. As such, culture is a seminally transformative force that, in its interplay with history and condition, has unparalleled ramifications on cognition, affect, relation, and therefore spirituality. In addition, culture stands in an inextricable dialectic with the forces of history and condition, and often provides the meaning lens through which history can be judged and condition can be assessed by the embedded subjectivity. Therefore, the dialectic between culture and subject is a third fundamental concern of Spiritual Leaders aiming to walk with clients as they Emerge. The objectification of the complexities of culture can be one of the most difficult endeavors in the Leadership relationship, since these constructs are deeply embedded in current-day subjectivities. Thus, whereas the effects of history's narratives and myths can be elucidated through a brand of incisive investigation, and condition's phase and stage determinations can be undertaken by examining age and life challenges, culture's constructs find themselves deeply enmeshed within the ontology of meaning itself, thereby removing any possibility of objectification through cognitive means alone. Cultural understanding and manipulation is the deepest of contextual spiritual arts, and therefore requires the gentle and knowing touch of a centered and prayerful Leader.

The Dimension of Context is the sum total of the background of any one person, the accretion of past stimuli, and the fundamental inheritance of the order of consciousness, as well as the extra-subjective complexities of current living that are influential upon subjectivity. As such, it is determinative of the subjective balances presented to the evolving spirit, and is a primary driver in both pathology and health models. And yet, the component of history *per se* is nothing other than the totality of the external story. Its counterforce, the internal story, is provided by the second element of Historical Space: the Dimension of Individuality.

b. Individuality: The Dimension of Height

In our discussion of subject-object theory, we highlighted the concept of identity as the unique shape that subjectivity takes in a particular meaning equilibrium. In that context, identity can be defined as one's self-concept, the constructed ideal of who I am in relation to what I know that I am not. In this context, however, I define the concept of Individuality as a person's social identity. As such, by Individuality I refer to one's placement within the matrix of the Dimension of Context. Hence, Individuality places itself within and stands in juxtaposition to the matrices of history, condition, and culture.

In his discussion of perception, Pierce developed a framework that I believe helps clarify what I am defining as Individuality. In his conception, Pierce stated that there are such things as first principles–effectual but unaffected, a force that exists *sui generis,* a grounding and a foundation, existence as existence. In our current discussion, the correlate to these first principles lies in the Dimension of Context, which outlines constructs and matrices into which subjectivity is embedded and out of which it makes meaning and functions. In addition, these matrices are external forces that are generally outside the control of subjectivity. As such, although they can be interpreted variously, they are not available to subjectivity's intentional agency. They are the first principles of Historical Space.

First principles, however, according to Pierce, are existent yet solitary and static, unless there is a 'something' against which they are can stand. This something is the juxtaposed presence of an Other. Since this Other is not a first principle, Pierce calls it a Second, and defines it as that which stands in juxtaposition to, or alongside of, a first principle. As such, this Second has not caused anything to happen nor has it interpreted its first principles. Rather, it is a Second in its fundamental existence, in its basic contra-distinction from first principles, and in its ability to somehow stand within and stand apart. Herein lies the basic nature of what I am defining as Individuality. I believe Individuality is the juxtaposition of subjectivity within the first principles of Context, where that subjectivity has not yet acted. In other words, Individuality is the Self that stands in the flow of Context's stream, and because of its juxtaposed identity alongside first principles (rather than being a first principle in and of itself), is the representative proponent of Seconds within Historical Space.[7]

As such, through the lens of the component of history, Individuality is the claiming of my unique place in the flow of time, as that flow of time interacts with my personal history. Individuality so conceived is the stipulation of my existence in light of my heritage, my ancestors, and my mythologies. It is the meaning-laden image I construct of myself in the panoply of those who have gone before me, who have lighted the road for me, who have solved mysteries before me, and who have defined my sense of connected pride. It is the sense of depth and entitlement that I bring to bear in my negotiation of my condition.

Individuality, through the lens of the component of condition, is defined as my construction of who I am in light of my age and my phase (stage apprehensions are often not conscious). As such, Individuality so conceived is the socially constructed self-concept I espouse as I work to overcome my life's challenges and progress through my psychosocial and societal responsibilities. Context-based Individuality is heavily influenced by the vagaries of the component of history (since historical formulations often set standards of success) as well as the preferences and biases of a particular society (since socially-based phase-appropriate standards infuse subjectivity). In other words, my conception of who I am, at this point in my life, as I compare myself to my historical and societal exigencies, makes up my context-based Individuality. Yet, within this Individuality are directional preferences that also affect social self-concept. The preferences are encapsulated in the culturally-based lens of Individuality.

Individuality, as conceived through the cultural lens, then, is the totality of the roles I can play, as I find my place in the various cultures in which I am engaged. As such, this lens on Individuality deals with personal constructions of how I can integrate with my social surround, how I am presented to my contextual condition, and how I prefer to interpret the exigencies of my culture. Therefore, the cultural lens of Individuality is aligned with the popular notion of personality, and is correspondingly modulated by the affective and social vagaries in the environment.

As such, the element of Individuality is a multi-faceted component of Historical Space. It involves the conception of who I am as I place myself in the matrix of my ancestors, my back narratives, my contextual

---

7. Pierce, *Collected Works*, 196.

phase, my subjective stage, and my cultural surround. It is therefore an externally-driven and holistic sense of an internally-driven personal distinctiveness, as that distinctiveness works to contribute in constructive ways to those same external contexts. It is the notion of existence in contra-distinction to the first principles of Historical Space—it is the element of Self that perceives Context and is aware that it is somehow different from it. As such, it is a stipulation of presence, a awareness of distinctiveness, and a complexification of existence. It is the agent, as agent, that stands in juxtaposition to Context, and is both a participant in and an observer of that Context. Spiritual Leaders are called to perceive this Individuality, as it makes itself seen against the backdrop of Context. Whereas Context provided information about the founding narratives and experiences of the Self, Individuality provides an impression of the Self that has found expression as a result of the concrescence of the vagaries of Context. We cannot understand a 'someone' without first grasping their background (Context); and also, we cannot grasp that same 'someone' without understanding that he or she stands in juxtaposition and relation to that Context (Individuality). As such, it is not simply the responsibility of Spiritual Leaders to assess Context. Rather, it is the responsibility of Spiritual Leaders to assess Individuality, in the light of Context.

And yet, the agent of which we speak, this Individuality, has not yet exerted its effect on or acted within Historical Space. Individuality so conceived is related only to subjectivity's existence, and not to its autonomous agency. For this crucial aspect of the very mechanics by which a person contributes to the social surround, I turn to the final element of Historical Space: the Dimension of Requisite.

c. Requisite: The Dimension of Length

We have already defined Context (the first principles of Historical Space) and Individuality (the Self that stands juxtaposed to those first principles). We have also stated that standing in juxtaposition to Context, Individuality has not yet exerted its agency in any way. It is the activity of Individuality (the exertion of its agency within Historical Space) that I refer to when I speak of the Dimension of Requisite. I define Requisite as the sum total of the acceptable and chosen behaviors in which one can engage, as one seeks to maintain position within, elucidate the meaning of, or make a contribution to Historical Space. Requisite is the accretion of chosen and developed rules of engagement, the various modes of interplay one chooses to cultivate, and the value basis through which a Self can move Individuality through its Context. As such, Requisite is how I strive for whatever it is I am striving for, how I define the limits of my interactions as I strive to further interact, and how I define my ideal of success as I strive to achieve my personal victories. Requisite so conceived is the concretization of all my spoken and unspoken norms of relational and contextual health, my conscious and non-conscious personal boundaries that guide my drives and needs, and my known or unknown benchmarks of personal progression through my historical narratives and social contexts. Therefore, if Context is encapsulated in the question 'where do I come from?', and Individuality in the question 'who am I in this place?', then Requisite is encapsulated by the question 'how am I to function?' The work of Spiritual Leaders is intimately intertwined with the conventions of Requisite. It is Requisite that introduces the personal principles of agency, the unique mechanics of interaction, and the particular behaviors that can or cannot find expression in the client's spirituality. As such, walking with clients as they toil to achieve Emergence implies a toiling through a particular repertoire of permitted activities and interactions. These activities and interactions are the very objects of Requisite and thereby form one of the fundamental pillars of client understanding, joining, and Leadership. Thus, it is not simply enough to understand where a clients comes from (Context). Nor is it enough to understand who a client is in within his or her Context (Individuality). Rather, the constructivist-developmental approach to Leadership stipulates that it behooves Leaders to correctly interpret, firmly grasp, and intimately dialogue with clients' constructed rules of engagement, as they interpret their position in relation to Context. As such, Spiritual Leaders must master the art of handling Context, Individuality, and Requisite—in short, the whole of Historical Space.

Historical Space in Action

The confluence of Context, Individuality, and Requisite gives a holistic conception of the notion of Historical Space, a complex and interlinked matrix of forces (analogous to the image of the jewels) in which each Dimension is complicit in and fundamentally affected by the staggering interrelations that form the whole. A solid grounding in the components and Dimensions of Historical Space is crucial to the Leader's ability to both comprehend the matrix within which the client is active, as well as the meanings presented by the client's subjectivity. Thus, Historical Space provides a strong indication of the possibilities and limits of a particular meaning-system. How so?

Historical Space, as with many other components of internal construction, is apprehended through subjectivity. And yet, its apprehension is never complete. In other words, there are always parts of Historical Space (and often significant parts) that are fused with subjectivity, that are non-conscious, that are tied to identity. As we mentioned earlier, because of subjective fusion, we cannot act upon that which is subject. At the same time, there are other parts of Historical Space that have undergone objectification, have become conscious, and can be effectively acted upon by subjectivity. As such, as we are confronted with clients, we are beset by two simultaneous and parallel incarnations of Historical Space. On the one hand, we find Objective Historical Space, which are all the elements of Context, Individuality, and Requisite that can be controlled, dissected, discussed, debated, and consciously transformed. In the investigation of the backgrounds and contexts of our clients, Spiritual Leaders will likely find themselves predominantly listening to and scrutinizing the conscious narratives of Objective Historical Space, as presented by clients. And yet, it should come as no surprise that these conceptions of history are but a portion of the story. The vast majority of Historical Space is held within the hidden complexities of Subjective Historical Space. Subjective Historical Space hides itself in the folds of clients' meta-narratives, betrays itself in clients' unwitting and autonomic behaviors, and exposes itself in clients' affective responses. As such, Spiritual Leaders must be attuned to the experience of clients, to the reactions and underlying substrates of meaning that drive those reactions, and to the bastions of value that clients are fiercely defending. It is in these hidden passageways of subjectivity that the majority of Historical Space is to be found. And it is through the practiced art of conversing and relating around these passageways, that the tenets and effects of Subjective Historical Space can be elucidated, understood, and transformed.

In addition to the Subject-Object balance inherent in Historical Space, there also is a dimension of value infusion in the understanding of clients with respect to the elements of Historical Space. Thus, all incarnations of Historical Space carry within them powerfully positive forces (those of inclusion, love, empowerment, self-regard, and confidence); these positive forces ground subjectivity in a world of support and good faith, confer value and importance to the Self, and act as anchors when direction and meaning seem to be lost. Directly juxtaposing these positive forces, and being derived from the same experiences of Historical Space, we find influential negative forces (destructive narratives, judgment, personal diminution, belittling, disenfranchisement, and unconstructive reasoning)—forces that are often the source of the drive for transformation, the basis of the desire for self-enhancement, and the impetus for movement and Emergence. It has been my experience, however, that these positive and negative forces come to the Leadership relationship as a consolidated whole, a completed package of personal history, and a collection of narratives that are difficult to dissect. In most of the cases that I have observed (both my own and those of my colleagues), I have found that this inextricability stems from the very personal and intense desire to maintain the growthful, nurturing, and grounding aspects of Historical Space. Without the attuned scrutiny of the shades of subjectivity, however, these positive aspects of Historical Space come to be intertwined and equated with the negative aspects. In other words, clients often begin by orienting themselves to Historical Space as if this Space is a consolidated and integrous whole, without internal division and devoid of compartmentalization. As a consequence, Spiritual Leaders are called to be exquisitely aware and deeply compassionate in their relations to clients, as the decrying of negative aspects of Historical Space can often be interpreted as an equivalent denigration of the positive aspects—aspects that clients are unwilling to release. As such, Spiritual Leaders must bear this Spatial dichotomy in mind, as they help clients objectify portions of Historical Space—aligning consciousness with the apprehension of the differences between negative and positive forces, and walking with clients as they re-balance subjectivity and recast alliances to Spatially held tenets.

In addition, these positive and negative forces interact with subjectivity in one of two main ways. First, with respect to Objective Historical Space complexities, the care seeker, being able to name and handle these complexities, will tend to view positive Historical Space forces as self-edifying, self-enhancing, and constructively healthy—the very list of his or her tradition and inheritance that is to be protected and fostered. As such, he or she will likely want to pursue the furtherance of these promotional messages as evolution and Emergence progress. Conversely, negative forces in Objective Historical Space will likely be reviled, distanced, and, in more extreme circumstances, rebelled against. Therefore, the care seeker will often labor to consciously rid himself or herself of these detrimentally-conceived forces, to turn away from that which is thought to be destructive, as disequilibrium brings about transformation. In response to these reactions, Spiritual Leaders have to be aware of the founding backgrounds that originated these biases in order to better be able to walk with and nurture the client through meaning re-equilibration and Emergence. Devoid an understanding of Objective Historical Space, these interrelated and fundamentally important forces could present themselves to the Spiritual Leader as a disconnected array of stimuli through which he or she will have to navigate blindly. And, the situation is even more tenuous in case of Subjective Historical Space.

In the case Subjective Historical Space, the care seekers cannot express or even perceive the effects of Historical Space on meaning construction and subjectivity. They are literally fused with this seminal portion of their spiritual story, they are personally defined by these narratives, and they soulfully relate to the various messages provided by myth, individuality, and engagement. As such, it falls to the Spiritual Leader to probe the motivations and non-conscious limits set by clients in order to help them make aspects of Subjective Historical Space object to the budding subjectivity. Incarnations of Subjective Historical Space are subtle, and are therefore difficult to perceive. In the subjective mode, positive forces of Historical Space are likely to be perceived as permission or internal drives toward particular ends that are intuited to be desirable. These are the very affective, relational, social and spiritual wants clients will be working toward. In effect, positive effects of Subjective Historical Space form one of the basic tenets of the *direction* that the clients hope transformation will take—the conception of the Self they would like to eventually be. Conversely, negative forces of Subjective Historical Space will often take the form of unnamed personal boundaries, limits on the horizons of possibilities that clients will allow or disallow themselves, a proverbial glass ceiling to conceptions of Selfhood and spiritual maturity. Therefore, Spiritual Leaders are confronted with the challenging and unique task of being present with clients as they work to objectify the source of these counteractive drives and limitations. In the subjective mode, drives and limitations are particularly frustrating and confounding to groping spiritualities. As such, the knowing, grounded, and oriented presence of the Spiritual Leader is critical in the constructive navigation of Subjective Historical Space, and therefore essential to the promotion of Emergence.

In sum, then, it is my belief that a primary goal of Spiritual Leadership is the ability to perceive and the knowledge of how to function within the Historical Space of the client—whether that Space is subject or object. In getting a handle on the client's meaning-making and construction mechanisms, Historical Space contributes the critical components of Context, Individuality, and Requisite, and interrelates these influences in a Whiteheadian construct of staggering complexity. As such, the importance of this Space cannot be underestimated. Scores of scholars—philosophical, psychological, sociological, theological, and pastoral—have attempted to understand this gargantuan concept, and marshal its tenets toward the constructive assistance of care seekers. Constructivist-developmentalism is no exception to this rule. One of the fundamental differences between other frameworks and constructivist-developmentalism, however, is that constructivist-developmentalism orients itself to the universal and dynamic. As such, by dealing with the ground of apprehension as well as its movement through evolution (rather than particular and static incarnations), this framework of Spiritual Leadership requires the Leader to be particularly attuned to the client's narrative—emotionally, intuitively, and most importantly, spiritually. It is through an act of therapeutic twinning, compassion, and *protection* that Spiritual Leaders can foster the constructive use of Historical Space within their clients. In addition, because of the relativized inter-relation of counselor and client, Leaders are called upon to develop a non-arbitrary framework through which they can help direct their clients and co-create the therapeutic culture of embeddedness. This concept of non-arbitrary protection is the second major goal of Spiritual Leadership.

2. TOWARD THE NON-ARBITRARY: PROTECTING THE CLIENTS' OPPORTUNITIES

Traditionally, the goals of the 'helping professions' have revolved around cultural and scientific norms of mental, emotional, and spiritual health. Every school of psychotherapeutic thought and practice, however, has propounded its version of what 'health' actually means. On one extreme, we have the traditional medical model—a diagnostic, labeling, stigmatized, and often medicating approach to moving a care seeker to mental health. On the other extreme, we find humanistic models (some of which go so far as to approximate tenets of new-ageism), stating that they orient themselves to the notions of wholistic health, to a person's strengths and balance, rather than only to illness, diagnosis, and medication. In both of these extremes, however, we find a common weakness: there is no accepted absolute standard of health against which these schools of thought can quantify their assertions of what makes up a state of health. In both cases, conceptions of healthiness are inevitably rooted in local cultures and epistemologies (in culturally influenced meaning-making), and are therefore little else than an incarnated reflection of the arbitrary biases of a particular group of people. Is it possible that, in their treatment of the norms of health, Spiritual Leaders could make pronouncements on the nature of spiritual health that are both specific and *non*-arbitrary? Is it possible for Spiritual Leaders to find an epistemological guidepost that would provide them with direction in their pursuit of the concepts of development and spiritual maturity? C.S. Pierce, the acclaimed father of semiology, made inroads at answering this difficult and mysterious question.

According to Pierce, all communication and apprehension is strictly semiological in nature, and therefore is fundamentally based on each person's abilities and preferences in decoding the messages received from all stimuli. Such a decoding is based on the individual's internal apprehension apparatus as it comes into dialogue with the complexities of experience. Thus, in his own way, Pierce was providing his definition for what we have been referring to as meaning-making. In so doing, he found himself mired in a world of relativity and became preoccupied with the question of how to find true objectivity in a world of individualized meaning. Undertaking a lengthy and ingenious philosophical discourse, Pierce drew his conclusion: according to him, true objectivity is that which would be glimpsed as a result of the agreement of an infinite number of minds working for an indefinite period of time. As such, although such a conception may sound too philosophical to be of any practical use, it highlights two important points about our conceptions of the nature of the non-arbitrary. First, Pierce's notion emphasizes the belief that the quest for true objectivity is an on-going human quest, one that will not end as long as there are humans.[8] Hence, the relativity of the

---

8. There is a strong relation here to Hegel's notion of Absolute Spirit. If we accept

lived world is subjugated to the overarching human progression toward an objectified agreement. Second, Pierce's notion provides a philosophical definition of a concept that humanity holds as intuitively correct: that despite our inexorable engagement in relativized meaning-making, we are still convicted in the notion that there is an objective reality outside of our individual consciousnesses, and that this reality is the ground from which justifications for the non-arbitrary stem.[9]

Harkening to Pierce's construct, I believe that the status of being an expert, in and of itself, confers no special validity on the values espoused and proclaimed, if these values are not supported by firm and generalized philosophical, scientific, and transcendent justifications. I believe that Spiritual Leaders often make pronouncements regarding the forms of spiritual health and that these pronouncements are nothing but arbitrary opinions unless they are intimately supported by psychological, philosophical, sociological, *and* theological considerations. Too often, I have been witness to a myriad of occasions in which a Spiritual Leader violated the sacred trust with his or her client by founding the process of the therapeutic relationship on arbitrary pronouncements of health. These pronouncements were invariably based on the Spiritual Leader's personal biases of security and safety. Pierce's notion of objectivity tells us, however, that, although purely non-arbitrary pronouncements are not possible by any single subjectivity, groundedness in a generalized community of diverse minds (both Scientific *and* Faithful) acts as a breakwater against which the waves of relativism are somewhat diffused and stripped of potency.

Adding a more practical spin to this discussion of objectivity, Kegan states that drawing conclusions on arbitrary bases leaves the door wide open to the introduction of the partialities of a given class, gender, religion, age, or culture. Consequently, despite claims to sophistication, what is considered illness is in grave danger of becoming nothing more than behavior that is frowned upon, or considered inconvenient, by the given population's proclivities. As such, conceptions of health can be reduced to behavior that is deemed acceptable and non-threatening by that same

---

the premise that all we can come to know is consciousness as it becomes aware of itself, then Pierce's assertion of the ever-progressive and never ending march toward objectivism is profound.

9. Pierce, *Collected Works*.

population.[10] In my opinion, this eventuality amounts to a demeaning of the human spirit and a violation of the tenets of Christianity. Arbitrary norms of health impose the limited meaning-making framework of the few on the developmental process of the many, make pronouncements of judgmental proportions on fellow human beings, create a hierarchy of the acceptability of each person's worth, broaden an unfair and self-serving power differential, foster a sense of exclusion within the client, and as such, threaten to violate the first Commandment.

In response to such damning charges, many in Spiritual Leadership have chosen to pursue an extreme client-centeredness—which is often expressed as a sort of utter non-direction (the discussion of whether this is even possible is a topic for another work). These Leaders have regarded the exercises of care for the client as including the temporary emersion in the client's struggle, as the client defines it. As a result, they stipulate their unwillingness to make a judgment on the client's situation in any way, regardless of the stated goals, beliefs or values of either the client or the Spiritual Leader. Pushed to its fullest incarnation, such a position places us firmly back in an anchorless world of pure relativism, thereby denuding the therapist of any ability to make helpful and constructive suggestions to the client regarding viable options for personal evolution. As such, the very notions of development, growth, and even maturity itself, lose their incisive salience. Donald Capps, in discussing the client-centered approach of counseling, affirms the inescapability of constructive pastoral diagnosis. He believes that complete non-direction (what he sees as a misapplication of the Rogerian framework) is not only impossible, but also destructive. Spiritual Leaders have powerful and seasoned insights to share with groping clients, as well as internal orientations that can help guide the culture of embeddedness in the direction of healing and away from the vagaries of confusion.[11] Spiritual Leaders also have a unique and needed insight into the personal struggles of each particular care seeker, information that is not readily available outside the counseling room. Thus, although the pursuit of non-direction respectfully and empoweringly places the client at the heart of the therapeutic engine, it does not provide a solid grounding from which to encourage and foster development, nor does it provide a useful counter-force in the creation of the client-Leader culture.

10. Kegan, *The Evolving Self*, 291.
11. Capps, *Living Stories*, 86.

Thus, as Kegan puts it: "The conviction that there are no non-arbitrary bases upon which to consider one state of meaning-making as better than another is, in a therapist, at once a philosophical confusion and a psychological confusion."[12] He continues to point out that, if we can work to resolve these confusions, through what I believe to be the openness of mind and study propounded by Pierce, a powerful stance arises: although Spiritual Leaders cannot make judgments on individuals as being more or less good than each other (this would be a direct violation of the Christian message), they are in a position to perceive some evolutionary equilibria as more or less constructive or adaptive than others. It is actually the differential between these evolutionary equilibrations that provides the basis from which to sense that spiritual counseling is moving toward Emergence.[13] Whether or not the Spiritual Leader voices the judgment of one stage over another is not necessarily a matter of mere personal justification to the client, but rather a matter of whether such an utterance would be received in a useful and growthful fashion by the client. Consequently, the Spiritual Leader can judge the process of the relationship according to whether the client is being presented with *opportunities* that, if capitalized upon, would lead the client to move from one order of consciousness to a more evolved one.[14]

I believe that the protection of this movement is the responsibility, concern, and goal of the Spiritual Leader. Therefore, in its very essence, Spiritual Leadership in the constructivist-developmental scheme addresses the client in the experience of the *on-going* process of meaning-making rather than in the static meaning the client has *already* made. It is a focus, basing itself on optimally non-arbitrary disciplines, on the process of evolution and not on the current spirituality in which clients find themselves. It is only through this responsible discipline to pursue non-arbitrary tenets of apprehension that a Spiritual Leader can truly

---

12. Kegan, *The Evolving Self,* 291.

13. Kegan, *In Over our Heads;* Peck, *Different Drum;* Capps, *Agents of Hope;* and Bacal et al., *Object Relations* also talk about therapists' experience of the relationship between themselves and their clients as being a valid and cogent source non-arbitrary information. It is non-arbitrary because it is fundamentally generative of the culture of embeddedness and determinative of the direction of insight. It must, however, be tempered by an artful engagement in counter-transference management. Counter-transference management is discussed in Chapter 6.

14. Kegan, *Evolving Self,* 292.

perceive and protect opportunities for growth throughout the client's quest.

Perceiving and protecting opportunities by fostering the attenuation of ever-more non-arbitrary apprehensions is the second major goal of the culture of embeddedness that must be created within the therapeutic relationship. But, what does the protection of opportunities imply about the *direction* of spiritual therapy? What are constructivist-developmental Spiritual Leaders hoping a client will do with his or her newly protected opportunities for growth? The answer is simple yet daunting: the constructivist-developmental Spiritual Leader is praying that the client will capitalize on these presented opportunities and, thus, set forward the motion of spiritual evolution. This activity of self-initialized growth I will refer to as self-determination. Helping clients transform their consciousness in order to acquire the capability of self-determination is the third major goal of the culture of embeddedness.

3. PROMOTING SELF-DETERMINATION

I remember a good friend of mine, a gentlemen of 74 years, saying to me that the hardest part of acclimatizing himself to his new bride was the breaking of his set in and cherished habits. In his admittedly hilarious account of his marriage, he talked about feeling like he was being broken in (like a horse), stripped of his much-loved old world machismo, and forced to maintain bounds of organization that he felt were nothing short of neurotic. Most importantly, he expressed sincere frustration and fear, because this relationship which had moved to an ever-heightened level of intimacy, was causing him to second guess his very notions of how to reason in the world, how to solve problems, and how to size people up. As such, although my dear friend expressed nothing but the deepest love for his new and admittedly charming bride, he was undergoing a meaning crisis that was based in the re-evaluation of all the supports he had built for himself, along with all the beliefs he had espoused regarding how the world works. We are not surprised to hear that marriage at later ages comes with its unique and pointed challenges. It is not, however, because it is hard to 'teach old dogs new tricks' (as my friend was fond of telling me). It is rather because the state of being an adult brings with it certain epistemological responsibilities that are difficult to counteract. Adults often come to us as closed systems.

In my experience, the vast majority of clients seeking the services of a Spiritual Leader are adults. The Spiritual Leadership of adults is a complicated affair because, as is clear from the story, adults come with vast complexes of interrelations and loyalties, of histories and futures, of achieved dreams and built hopes, and of conceptions of efficacious methods of orienting the Self through life's challenges and triumphs—methods that have been developed through hard work and considerable spiritual labor. They are often aware of the subtext of why they have sought Spiritual Leadership, as well as a hopeful desire for a particular resolution to the presenting problem. As such, they present a double-edged experience for Leaders: it is not uncommon for a Spiritual Leader to have ambivalent and cautious feelings when confronted with such a complex client. In my experience, for every Spiritual Leader who is enchanted by the facility of an adult client to reason and to risk, there is another Leader who is deeply frustrated by the hard and fast imprinted meanings the adult has learned and is unwilling to transform or relinquish. For every Spiritual Leader who gleams at the eagerness and self-possession of an adult client, there will be another who will be lead through the maze of the various forms of empiricism and personal defense, which unwaveringly supersede questions of philosophy or theology and out of which the client refuses to venture.

Yet, I believe that we must ensure that our stipulations of the goals of Spiritual Leadership attend and respond constructively to the needs and situations of our adult clients, who don't necessarily afford themselves the luxury of learning and growing for the pure sake of learning and growing. Adults are notorious for expending energy on endeavors (including therapy and Spiritual Leadership) only when they are convinced of the endeavor's relevance to their daily lives and to the progression toward their particular goals. As such, it is the fostering of an adult person's ability to pursue these personal goals and to integrate them into the framework of arising subjectivities, undertaken through the impetus of his or her personal and contextual agency, that is a basic goal of constructivist-developmental Spiritual Leadership. In light of this, I believe that the third major goal of Spiritual Leadership is to create an environment in which the client can come to be self-determinative, responsibly and autonomously growth- and integration-oriented, and equipped to deal with the vagaries of personal transformation. In other words, as

Spiritual Leaders, we need to do our jobs so well, that we render our services obsolete.

I define self-determinative people as those who have developed the internal impetus and spiritual tools required to Emerge. Self-determination is a practiced and focused teleological application of spirit—a progressive and internal claim to the evolution of one's personal order of consciousness. As such, self-determination implies a congruent ability to decipher personal desire, values, and impressions, from societally-, historically-, or culturally-prescribed messages. It is an evocative owning of one's meaning-constitutive processes and a loving nurturance of spirituality. Therefore, self-determinative people can perceive and judge the incongruence between their lived experiences and their desired Selves, between their social effects and their desired social identities, and between their existential anxieties and their desired state of spiritual peace. In addition, self-determinative people have the internal energetic and affective impetus to resolve that incongruence. In short, self-determination is the power to vision goals and the competent drive to achieving those goals. As such, it requires a probing spirit, individual awareness, a communal identity, an open heart and an open mind. Self-determinative people develop an identifiable sense of connection with the Ultimate, as they expand a sense of themselves as co-creators of the culture that shapes them, and of the forces that guide them. They are characterized by the ability to take responsibility for beliefs and relationships, to set spiritually-congruent standards of acceptability, to take action, and to freely assess the progression of Selfhood. Consequently, self-determination is an exigency of adult, Western, post-modern living, and therefore, reflects a primary thrust, and a fundamental cultural impetus that cuts across all areas of adult life.

If self-determination is culturally encoded in the exigencies of Western adult life, why is it so infrequently encountered? Why is so much time spent (in healing relationships) in the construction of self-determination? Why do we not see it arise spontaneously in the larger adult population? In my opinion, there are two answers: first, the order of consciousness required for unilateral self-determination is one that tends to arise in adulthood, and only after deliberate cultivation; and second, over the course of our lives, we are simply not taught to be self-determinative.

As with all internal spiritual processes, orders of consciousness complexify as they evolve, reaching into ever more abstract corners of the human experience, and promoting ever greater subjective attenuation and objective perception. As such, moving through a Piagetian construct of qualitative re-definition (decentration), these orders of consciousness transform from those which are focused on impulses and immediate need satisfaction on the one extreme (often seen in the typical tantrum throwing two year old), to those that are focused on universal morality, principles of truth, and chosen systemic detachment on the other. Between these two poles are several stages of increasing complexity, as consciousness works to grasp its world and stabilize itself. The order of consciousness required for self-determination does not arise until after the interpersonal preoccupations of teenage and university are weathered and conquered.[15] As such, the maturity of spirit required for self-determination, although it is something that is ubiquitously encouraged throughout high school years and early adulthood, is not truly animate until interpersonal preoccupations are subsumed to drives of personal autonomy and authority. In short, until a person has completed university, it is rare to find true self-determination possible within consciousness. As such, many adults seeking spiritual care have only just developed the consciousness capacity to exhibit self-determination—a capacity that has not likely been cultivated in the absence of a mentoring education. As such, Spiritual Leaders dealing with adults and working to co-create a culture of embeddedness that promotes self-determination may find that they are breaking relatively untouched ground within the client's developing spirituality. To that end, much gentility, patience, and compassion will need to be invoked to keep the Spiritual Leader centered and receptive, as the client works to develop what might otherwise be considered a simple reality of maturity. And yet, the simple reality evades many of us in society until we are aided through the process. It is my belief that this evasion is the result of my second reason for the dearth of self-determination in adult society: we are simply not taught to be self-determinative.

From the instant we are born, we typically find ourselves in the care of authoritative figures that know more about us, about the world,

---

15. For more on stage theory, please see Fowler, *Stages of Faith*; Kegan, *Evolving Self*; Kohlberg, *Moral Stages*; Erikson, *Childhood and Society*; Piaget, *Constructions of Reality*; Perry, *College Years*.

about dangers, and about pleasures than we do. Consequently, we invest ourselves in following the preferences and wills of these Big People, who seemingly take care of the difficult details of life while we simply explore our environments and gain a sense of personal stability. Of course as this story is extended, we find that, generally speaking, we are handed off to a long line of authority figures: from parents to early childhood educators; from early childhood educators to elementary teachers; from elementary teachers to secondary school teachers; from secondary school teachers to a vast array of tutors, coaches, and mentors; from these influential figures to professors; and from professors to bosses, while all the while retaining a degree of relation with our primary care takers. This is a long history of heteronymous compliance and an inheritance of obedience and deference. In fact, non-compliance often results in scathing, socially-embarrassing, and disconnecting punishments—often providing a negative example to others who might wish to rebel, strike out, or stand alone. The legacy of such a background is not difficult to see: although the demands of modern Western life require an order of consciousness capable of self-determination, adults arrive at this critical juncture denuded of history, example, tools, or direction on how to function in such a level of spirituality. As such, the movement from quasi-self-determination, which most often is nothing other than the veiled rebellion of young adulthood (rebellion being nothing other than behaviors chosen to deliberately counteract preset, accepted conventions—a shielded expression of a life Other-controlled), to true self-determination is an emergent evolution that requires the caring aid of a practiced and loving hand—the hand of a knowing Spiritual Leader.

Therefore, if the aim of Spiritual Leadership is the aim of fostering the evolved spirituality, which enables self-determination, Spiritual Leaders are then called to a strict and stringent non-arbitrary protection of the opportunities for growth toward that sophistication of spiritual expression. As such, Spiritual Leaders are exonerated from the inappropriate intra-therapy conflict of choosing between the practical and the theological preferences of a client's epistemology (a practice that goes strictly against client-centered and humanistic approaches to healing). Rather, if the Spiritual Leader would seek to walk with the client and protect his or her opportunities for growth so that the client might achieve the order of consciousness necessary for self-determination, this forms the basis of a powerful way of attending to the needs of adult clients, as they work to navigate the considerable complexities of their lives. The goal of Spiritual Leadership, then, is not so much a matter of getting the client to identify and value distinctions between the conflicting parts within and making judgments on those distinctions, but rather a matter of fostering a qualitative evolution of consciousness—literally a heightened spirituality—which supports and creates those very distinction.[16]

Spiritual Leaders seeking to help their clients toward self-determination, then, are essentially nurturing them to transform their fundamental subjectivities and meaning-constructions, by helping them come to terms with their personal power and the limits of their autonomy, the boundaries of the influences of their worlds, and their chosen reactions to the vagaries of personal relationships. They are asking clients to put aside the no-longer-useful adherences to the foundations of their current heteronymous constructions of empowerment, in favor of new and emergent loyalties—internally driven, spiritually-motivated, and meaning-constitutive. This is often a long and truly painful process for the client, a process that will repeat itself at various heights of abstractness throughout the whole course of life. Because of the frustration and recrimination characteristic of transformative interactions, the process may not be perceived by the client as a triumph of spirit, regardless of the Spiritual Leader's encouragement and presence. And yet, self-determination is a fundamental driver of phase-appropriate, responsible adult functioning, and a foundational tenet of spiritual movement and maturity.[17] It is in light of this that I restate my belief in the goals of Spiritual Leadership: to walk with, nurture and hold our clients as they struggle painfully to make new meaning of their lives, while at the same time non-arbitrarily protecting their opportunities for growth and evolution into the order of consciousness that allows for self-determination. Ironically, we are victorious when we are no longer required.

---

16. Kegan, *In Over Our Heads*, 275.

17. Fowler believes, in his elucidation of the stages of faith development, that the ability to be self-determined is a fundamental requirement for a mature spirituality. Without such an ability, he believes that spirituality cannot grow beyond its lower and prescribed stages, and therefore remains predominantly heteronymous, unscrutinized, and unchosen.

4. FOSTERING INSIGHT

The elucidation of the effects of Historical Space and the eventual decision for what to do about its lingering effects do not arise spontaneously from the Spiritual Leadership relationship alone. In fact, such difficult and personal decisions arise out of the client's ability to mine the impetus presented by the appearance of insight. Insight development is a fundamental event in the progression of healing within the client. As such, this section, the final section in our discussion of the goals of Spiritual Leadership, outlines the important and seminal contribution of insight to the progression of spiritual evolution.

If the Spiritual Leader takes a long-sighted view of the sacred process of spiritual evolution, not only will he or she attend to the present evolutionary situation but also to every subsequent one, as each learning situation is the base for the next. The growth situation itself will carry within it several aspects: that which is known, that which is not known, and that which is problematic.[18] The confluence of these three aspects, under a proper and prayerful process, can lead the client to a place of new understanding. This new understanding, this emergent awareness, is what I refer to as insight. Insight, then, is the energetic force that drives evolution.

According to Lonergan, insight has three main characteristics: it comes as a release due to the attention of inquiry; it comes suddenly and somewhat unexpectedly; and it occurs between the concrete and the abstract levels of awareness.[19] I will discuss each of these characteristics separately.

In the first characteristic, the release Lonergan speaks of is the release from biological drives, emotional subjectivities, habitual processes, and meaning routines. The release brings with it the re-emergence of a sense of wonder and often an increased desire to learn more. It is the momentum of this release that I believe can be transformed into the impetus for further growth in the therapeutic spiritual relationship. I have said that I believe one of the goals of Spiritual Leadership to be the non-arbitrary protection of opportunities for the transformation of the consciousness of the client. As such, the emergence of impetus introduced by insight is a powerful tool in the forward motion of the

---

18. Richmond, *Piaget*, 91.
19. Lonergan, *Insight*, 3.

evolution of the client's order of consciousness. Therefore, as a corollary to the protection of opportunities, I believe that Spiritual Leaders must be attuned to the heightened energy that arises after the discovery of an insight. This is an energy that can be hedged against the human tendency to wallow after a victory has been won. In their quest to non-arbitrarily protect the opportunities for transformation, I believe that Spiritual Leaders must also encourage their clients to capitalize on the energy that makes itself available throughout the course of therapy. In so doing, not only are the clients aided in their perceptions of the power of insight, but also in their capacities to exploit its impetus. It is in this way that Spiritual Leaders can further the third goal of Spiritual Leadership: the encouragement of the client to become self-determined.

Lonergan's second characteristic of insight speaks of the sudden and often unexpected appearance of insight. In fleshing out his thoughts, he claims that insights are often begun by an intuition, a suggestion, a subtle clue buried somewhere in the awareness of the seeker. In following the string of this intuition, clients lead themselves to a space in which an old awareness breaks down and a new awareness breaks through. These are the moments Eugene Gendlin refers to as experiences of 'internal shift'.[20] On the road to this shift, Gendlin discusses the weaving in and through the subtle shades and colors that make up our consciousness. In his paradigm, the act of sitting and internally searching leads to a naming of the clue presented by intuition. The act of naming brings about insight and internal systemic relief, and thereby results in the release outlined by Lonergan. As a witness to this exploration, Spiritual Leaders are asked to patiently hold the client as he or she progresses through the sacred activity of self-scrutiny and self-definition. This is often an unsure and embarrassing time for the client as he or she comes face-to-face with a less mature and less integrous form of the Self—a form which until now has been obvious to everyone but the client. The exposition of this form is a moment of utmost importance as it hangs the question of personal acceptability in the very balance of the therapeutic relationship. Consequently, I believe it is the Spiritual Leader's responsibility to be attentive to these emotions and to gently and patiently hold the client through this often discomforting and naked transition.

As a corollary to the first two characteristics, Lonergan's third characteristic speaks of insight as taking place between the concrete and the

20. Gendlin, *Focusing*, 50.

abstract. He goes on to explain that the convergence of concrete and abstract, much like the convergence of Science and Faith, creates the victory of a balanced achievement. By the cooperation of these forces, then, successive adjustments, questions and answers, the known and the understood, the image and the concept all converge to present a solid front of knowing which propels evolution forward. Yet, as we know from our earlier discussion, the breaking through of an intuition is not enough to effect transformation. A qualitative transformation of consciousness cannot come simply through the realm of the cognitive, but must speak to spirituality, which is prior to cognition. As such, all the elements of consciousness, concrete and abstract, must be brought to bear by the client in the final accommodation of insight that will lead to transformation. Malone and Malone point out that thought, behavior, emotion, relation, and spirit in their *full congruency* must necessarily attend to an insight in order for it to become a transformative experience.[21] Consequently, Spiritual Leaders are confronted with a difficult and focused task: they are called upon to hold and recognize the various levels of the client's Self that make their appearances. Through this validation, the various levels of being are encouraged to remain visible and to weigh in, in their respective fashions, on the insight being considered. Therefore, Spiritual Leaders further protect the opportunities for the client's growth by encouraging the various internal voices of the client to remain at the table as the negotiation of evolution takes place. In relying on the Spiritual Leader to effectively manage this task, the client is now freer to devote his or her energies to the process of equilibrating meaning-making as well as to the process of observing himself or herself as the new structures are built through objectification. The final result is the increased awareness of the client and the greater likelihood that he or she will be able to engage in such activities in the future: in short, they are a step closer to self-determination.

In summary, a constructivist-developmental approach to Spiritual Leadership investigates and interprets Historical Space in order to enhance joining and grasp the client's spiritual discourse and inheritance; using this information as a relational lens, Spiritual Leadership pursues the non-arbitrary protection of opportunities for growth that will usefully assist the client in achieving spiritually-transforming insight; as this transformation is progressing, Spiritual Leadership encourages a

21. Malone and Malone, *The Windows of Experience*, 37.

culture of embeddedness and an order of consciousness within the client that moves toward further self-determination, thereby forestalling the development of therapeutic dependency and furthering an autonomous, integrated and advanced level of spiritual awareness.

In light of the deep, other-centered, and artful nature of such endeavors, Spiritual Leaders would do well to engage in a movement toward construction and away from instruction. Through the co-mingling of the dual creation that is the therapeutic relationship, clients can weather disequilibrium and begin to lead new, more articulated, better-organized constructions of reality, which differentiate and reintegrate the understanding of the prior equilibrium. In addition, this formulation reinforces the notion that crises cannot simply be arbitrarily categorized as illness. Breakdowns in meaning-making are not automatically pathological; in the vast majority of cases, breakdowns in meaning-making are the hallmarks of transition—and transitions are the driving forces of consciousness evolution and Emergence. The Spiritual Leader stands as a witnessing partner to the whole and holy process.

5

Creating Environment

THE ENVIRONMENT OF THE CULTURE OF EMBEDDEDNESS

I HAVE COVERED THE first element of the culture of embeddedness: the goals of Spiritual Leadership (the investigation of Historical Space, the non-arbitrary protection of the client's transformation opportunities, the movement toward self-determination, and the cultivation of insight). The pursuit of these goals, however, must take place within a context, which is conducive to transformative growth. As such, in order to elucidate this context, I will now turn my attention to the environment necessary for constructive Spiritual Leadership, as seen through the lens of constructivist-developmentalism. In the process of exploring issues of the culture of embeddedness, I will use examples that reference children. I ask my reader to recall, however, that the fundamental movement of growth, evolution, and Emergence is a movement that is universally and uniformly undertaken by persons at every age. Therefore, I use examples referencing childhood as metaphors for the interaction between adults. I have judged this as the best course of action since the illustrations of the development of childhood are less abstract than those involving adults and are therefore more useful in our exploration as we elucidate the construction of a culture of embeddedness.

In his elucidation of the 'holding environment', Winnicott asserted that infant maturation is a cultural and environmental undertaking, wherein the infant's primary caretakers provide the environmental and affective impetus under which the infant develops and comes to know the world. The same notion is true of the Spiritual Leadership relationship: the care seeker is never transforming in a vacuum. Just as the infant's caretaker is more than simply the bringer of sustenance, but rather the very environment out of which the infant differentiates, so the therapeutic relationship with the Spiritual Leader is more than simply a safe place: it creates the context through which transformation will or will not flourish. In other words, the Spiritual Leadership relationship, much like the infants primary caretaker, will provide the fundamental psychosocial context necessary for the client's evolving equilibria.

The psychosocial environment is the particular form of the world in which a person is embedded, at a particular point in time. Therefore, it is the very context in which and out of which a person grows. As such, far from being a formless environment, the psychosocial context shapes and defines the fundamental structures of meaning-making and subject apprehension. In addition, it defines these structures in the direction of the combined meaning-making of its originators. As such, it is a directional, stable construct and a ubiquitous influence that enters into a dialogue with subjectivity. It is therefore analogous to a culture. Consequently, the constructivist-developmental school commonly refers to it as the culture of embeddedness.

The culture of embeddedness is not a concept that is limited to the formational stages in a person's life, however. Every stage we enter, every life phase we complete, and every moment we invoke consciousness is essentially and deeply affected by our cultural surround (as illustrated by the complexities of Historical Space). As adults, having developed a degree of agency and autonomy, we contribute to the culture of embeddedness in a much more explicit way than did the figurative infant. In fact, as voice and agency increase, we contribute in a more and more executive fashion to the formation of this culture. As such, we become co-creators of that in which we are embedded, architects of the forces from which we draw influence, and contributors to the shape of our social surround.[1] In addition, these cultures of embeddedness evolve with us throughout our lifecycle—being moulded by the varying exigencies of context, Emergence, and life phase. In other words, there is not a single culture of embeddedness, but many.[2] These cultures are the psychosocial environments that draw us in and include us, as well as those that challenge us and allow us to differentiate. Thus, according to Mackie and many other sociological scholars, what Winnicott says of

---

1. This is analogous to a social version of Absolute Spirit.
2. Kegan, *Evolving Self,* 116.

the infant is true of all of us, at all points in our lives.³ Individuals never stand in isolation—we are never alone unto ourselves. We are the very embodiment of our environmental matrices. A healthy Self, then, is the congruent presence of both the differentiated side of the individual and the socialized, acculturated side.

According to Piaget, growth activities, which increase differentiation and acculturation, cannot occur without interchange between an individual and his or her surroundings: both processes are paramount to the construction of a coherent Self.⁴ He believes that in order for development to occur, there must be action upon the culture by a Self and a resultant counteraction upon the Self by the culture. In fact, this process is the very foundation of the concepts of Accommodation and Assimilation described earlier. The implication is that a client's passive presence with the Spiritual Leader will not assist transformation in the order of consciousness, any more than watching a group of objects will lead to knowledge of their interrelations. Social interaction, then, whether with a single person or a group of people, implies a situation in which the meaning constructions of each member actively co-create the resultant relationships and culture. Through the continued interaction with this culture, a person must invoke the capacities to assimilate and accommodate stimuli so as to find more constructive and healthy equilibria for meaning-making. As such, a person further develops Selfhood. Therefore, the importance of the type of culture of embeddedness that is created is paramount to the success of the attempts the client makes toward spiritual growth.

What are the responsibilities of the Spiritual Leader in the co-creation of this culture of embeddedness? I believe the answer is three-fold: the Spiritual Leader must hold the client inclusively, empathically, and compassionately in order to foster a sense of unthreatened belonging and safety, within which the current equilibrium can exist peacefully; at the same time, the Spiritual Leader must gently and productively contradict and challenge the client, at the client's particular stage of meaning-making, in order to encourage differentiation and confront neurotic incarnations of comfort; finally, throughout the entire process, the Spiritual Leader must co-create the culture of embeddedness such that the client is certain that the Leader will not abandon him or her before the achieve-

3. Mackie, *Constructing Men and Women*, 62.
4. Boden, *Piaget*, 95.

ment of re-equilibration. Thus, the client will feel more free to risk and to divest himself or herself of old patterns without the fear of rejection, loneliness, solitude, or destructive self-doubt.[5] Environments that are weighted too heavily in the Direction of Inclusion risk encouraging a sense of complacency and dependency within the client and, as such, are a violation of the stated goals of Spiritual Leadership. Environments that are weighted too heavily in the Direction of Contradiction encourage self-recrimination and self-judgment within the client, who may feel attacked and challenged at the most fundamental levels of his or her being. Thus, such environments amount to nothing more than a veiled abandonment of the client by an over-zealous Spiritual Leader. Environments that promote the fear of abandonment within the client encourage and foster the deepest forms of self-protection and defensiveness, thereby reducing the relationship to a distrustful tug-of-war between client and Leader. Consequently, the resultant culture is in direct contradiction to Christ's teachings with respect to loving our neighbors. The constellation of subtle activities required of the Spiritual Leader, then, amount to a careful confluence of art and technique, Faith and Science, 'Me' and 'I', all of which are steeped in the unmistakable gentility of Christian love.

The Direction of Inclusion

The first function of a healthy culture of embeddedness is the function of inclusion, empathy, and compassion. These elements, crucial to the development of humanity from infancy onward, are the ground of a paramount aspect of any growthful relationship: attachment.[6] The experience of attachment is directly related to how a person comes to know the Self, comes to view the Self's worth, comes to understand the factors at play in the environment with respect to the Self, and comes to grasp the personal agency the Self has in the shaping of those external factors. Some of the strongest and most common negative emotions brought forward in a therapeutic relationship are the harmful emotions that stem

---

5. This is an environmental construction that spans many schools of therapy and counseling. In the constructivist-developmental framework, however, its application is particular. The purpose of this section is to elucidate this application. For other applications of this approach, please see Kegan, *In Over Our Heads*; _____, *Evolving Self*; Whitehead, *Process and Reality*; Hegel, *Phenomenology Of Mind*; Malone and Malone, *The Windows of Experience*; Capps, *Living Stories*; Goldberg, *Speaking with the Devil*; and Goleman, *Social Intelligence*.

6. Kegan, *The Evolving Self*, 124; see also Bowlby *Attachment*; Sullivan, *Psychiatry*.

from neurotic and persistent feelings of unworthiness, loneliness, and impotence. According to attachment theory, these are the emotions that are counteracted by a solid and unwavering attachment to primary caregivers.[7] In other words, a child's experience of attachment to his or her primary caregivers is the very ground of emotional security and comfort, the basis of self-regard and self-confidence, as well as the foundation of the orientation toward the spiritual aspects of life. The attitudes that we adopt toward our feelings, therefore, are socially constructed between the child and the caregiver. Children learn to soothe themselves as they have been soothed, to motivate themselves as they have been motivated, and to love themselves as they have been loved. Since the relationship with the caregiver creates the culture of embeddedness, much like Historical Space, this culture becomes an active agent in formation, an evolutionary anchor, so to speak, an exemplar of Winncott's holding environment. Thus, we are formed by our relationship to that within which we are included, and to that with which we allow ourselves to be fused.

The constructivist-developmental view carries this pattern of infancy into the furthest reaches of adult life. Attachment theory in and of itself states that, in the moderate failure of proper attachment in childhood, care seekers can find a degree of healing through the forging of truly attuned and attached relationships, even in adulthood. As such, attachment-oriented therapists are very concerned with the development of a truly inclusive, safe, and nurturing therapeutic holding environment, as they counsel their clients and promote affective and spiritual healing.[8] Constructivist-developmentalism believes that this culture of inclusion is much more than an affective intervention. Rather, it is paramount to the very formation of spiritual equilibria at all stages in one's life span. Consequently, Spiritual Leaders are called upon to, first and foremost, foster this sense of true and sincere attachment, as it is the very ground of the client's future strength and impetus. Much like the infant with his or her caregiver, I believe that the client relies on the Spiritual Leader to act as a mirror of the client's worth, beauty, power, and fundamental acceptability.[9] This attachment must pervade the relationship and not waver during moments of tension or negativity.

---

7. Barnet and Barnet, *The Youngest Minds*, 67 and Bowlby, *Attachment*.
8. Bacal and Newman, *Object Relations*, 56–74.
9. For more on mirroring and its importance, please see Kohut, *The Analysis of Self*.

Emotions of tension and negativity will occur frequently throughout the course of the therapeutic relationship, as they are often the primary reason for which the client is seeking help. Michael Nichol states that these emotions are difficult to weather, even as a witness, and as such, are often unwittingly dispelled by the Spiritual Leader, therapist, or helper by practices of denial, rationalization, or dismissal.[10] For example, it is not uncommon to hear a listener or care giver deflect the pain presented by a speaker by engaging in problem-solving discourse ("Have you ever thought of…?" or "What you should do is…"), or in distraction mechanisms, such as relating one's own similar story ("I know exactly what you mean. That reminds of the time when…"). It should be explicitly noted, however, that these reactions are not carried out with an intent to sabotage—far from it. Rather, it is my experience that these reactions can occur for two main reasons: on the one hand, the anxiety the listener feels at helplessly witnessing his or her counterpart suffer acts as a spur to a simple, almost autonomic affective response—the desire, usually stemming from a genuine concern for the other, to alleviate the pain we are witnessing as quickly as possible; on the other more sinister hand, the anxiety the listener feels at hearing the care seeker's pain results from the listener's personal inability to manage and coordinate such intense emotionality within himself or herself (a common affective and relational trap that can only be remedied through careful and lengthy rounds of self-awareness and spiritual growth activities).[11] Thus, in working to promote this pain alleviation, listeners, care-givers, and counselors risk to hamper the listening process and to disallow the anxious speaker to utterly own the anxiety he or she is trying to frame and overcome.

In discussing this problematic response, I believe that such actions strip the care seeker from the permission to express and experience his or her unique condition, and are, as such, fundamental breaches in the fabric of spiritual becoming. Such breaches literally render the care seeker invisible within the matrix of the relationship, disallowing honest emotionality and self-being (the fundamental drivers of the therapeutic energy economy). In addition, such breaches not only disallow congru-

---

10. Nichols, *The Lost Art of Listening*, 95.

11. For more on this relational trap, please see Nichols, *The Art of Listening*. There is also a very interesting discussion of the role of borrowed shame in listeners in Goldberg, *Speaking with the Devil*.

ent self-expression on the part of the client but also replace it with an externally-imposed construction of the care seeker's identity but the defending subjectivity—that of the Spiritual Leader. Consequently, no space is left in the culture of embeddedness for growth: if we cannot honestly and openly bring forward that which requires transformation, how can transformation be effected? Therefore, I believe that such harmful actions unwittingly and destructively bring the therapeutic culture of embeddedness to the defense of the current (and no longer viable) evolutionary equilibrium, thereby thwarting the client's stimulus and tragically eradicating the client's opportunities for growth. Throughout this doomed defense, the Spiritual Leader is relating to the client as the 'individual in the current state of meaning' rather than to the 'Self as the constant motion of meaning-making'.[12] In other words, this practice amounts to a protection of made-meaning rather than the promotion of the evolutionary experience of meaning transformation. It guides the client to hold on to the status quo rather than to pursue Emergence. The danger of such a practice, in my opinion, is that it encourages the client to conclude that experiences of discomfort, of 'not-me', are experiences to be defended against, somehow corrected, and finally dismissed rather than plunged into, integrated, and transformed. Or worse yet, it disallows a transformation-ready client from finding the relational impetus and cultural energy required to truly Emerge. In either case, the unfortunate client, although he or she may feel deeply cared for by the Spiritual Leader's genuinely warm demeanor, will not achieve insight, will not recognize the presented opportunities for growth, and will not learn to become self-determined. In short, he or she will not Emerge.

In contrast, when Spiritual Leaders respond, not to the problem as problem but to the transforming person as the process of experiencing Emergence through the problem, the client is acknowledged as acceptable, visible, worthy, and understandable (despite the inevitable negative emotions that likely abound). Furthermore, and most importantly, the client is acknowledged as the 'ever-progressive motion of spirit', a motion that cannot be denied without cost, a motion that includes experiences of balance and imbalance, each as an intrinsic and inescapable part of an integrous and evolutionary life. In addition, this attitude testifies to the client's dignity, power, and self-determination, while simultaneously reinforcing feelings of constancy, attachment, and basic trust in the Self

12. Kegan, *The Evolving Self*, 125.

and in the process of transformation and Emergence. Therefore, the inclusion function of Spiritual Leadership promotes holding qualities in the culture of embeddedness by attending to, recognizing, seeing, and validating the client as a worthy, competent, and loveable person, despite the often confusing and recriminating feelings that might grip the client's heart.

But, as we have already stated, inclusion is not enough to promote spiritual evolution. As in the Pentateuchal narrative, the impetus for growth is presented by the presence of opposition. It is to this issue that I turn my attention in the next section.

The Direction of Contradiction

I was once lined up at a food court counter, waiting patiently for my turn to buy an ice-cream cone. As I stood, I was astounded by the impressive array of novel and creative ice cream flavors presented by this particular chain. I was quietly making my selection, when the lady in front of me decided to allow her two year old son, Tommy, to choose his own ice cream flavor. My first thought was that this was a charming display of a doting mother trying to teach her child a degree of autonomy. But then I realized that the situation was very different indeed: this mother stood there before the two dozen flavors of ice cream and proceeded to read each and every name to her increasingly confounded looking son. She then waited for his answer, and punctuated his long, awkward, and bewildered silence with the occasional, "So? What do you think, Tommy?"

It occurred to me at that point that what I was witnessing was not the story of a mother teaching her son about autonomy and decision-making. Parents tend to have an intuitive sense of their children's cognitive capabilities and a twenty-four month old child is simply unable to assimilate two dozen options of anything, let alone exotic ice cream flavors. Rather, what I was witnessing was a mother, so concerned about showing her son how much she loved him, that she was unwilling (or perhaps even unable) to set appropriate boundaries to help guide Tommy in a phase-appropriate fashion. Eventually, the deadlocked conversation was set in motion again by the clever store clerk who, smiling, turned to the befuddled looking boy and said, "Hey Tommy, how about some delicious chocolate?"

In my estimation, people in Western society are not comfortable dealing with concepts such as personal power, authority, and accountable charge, especially when they are asked to be introspective about the intimate relationships in their lives (this is presumably due to a combination of personal humility, a sense of personal ineptitude, and a disdain for how they have witnessed such power and charge being used in the past). Responsible and compassionate expressions of power, authority and charge are especially important in the lives of youngsters like Tommy, who require a competent executive force overseeing them, and a sure sense that a trustworthy 'someone' is in charge of the vagaries of life—setting boundaries, monitoring permissions, providing protection, and fostering maturity. Piaget believed that these forces are paramount because children are constantly engaged in the process of learning to take charge of their impulses and needs, to exercise control over themselves in more sophisticated ways. As such, they learn to pursue their own goals and aspirations with a new and greater measure of independence and autonomy, and consequently, take greater ownership and pleasure in partaking of the relationships and activities they co-created.[13] Hence, power, expressed as responsible boundary setting, must cut in two counter-balanced directions: one the one hand, boundary setting is the process by which we disallow a particular behavior (or behavior class) because we deem it to be less than optimally constructive; on the other usually less acknowledged hand, boundary setting involves the continuous encouragement of particular behaviors, a sort of positive discipline and guidance meant to shape behavior toward desired ends. The boundary in this case is subtle: the act of encouraging behavior in a particular direction implies the decision *not* to encourage it from moving in another direction (a behavioral and educational parallel to the meaning-making process). As such, in conjunction with the embracing effects of constructive inclusion, boundary setting and the responsible use of power are fundamentally important for the development of a growthful holding environment.

These same tenets hold true for the development of care-giving as seen through the constructivist-developmental framework of spiritual growth, and are therefore foundational to the Spiritual Leader's approach. It is not possible for Spiritual Leaders to avoid the use of power in their relationships. As with all invested interactions, each member of the relationship is determinative of the course the affiliation will take, as well as determinative of its potentialities and outcomes. In addition, Spiritual

---

13. Richmond, *Piaget*, 100.

Leaders, by virtue of their titles, social position, and education-level, are commonly viewed as knowledge-based, and practice-oriented authority figures. As such, they are immediately and intimately infused with an aura of power by many care seekers—an aura that must be honored, on the hand, and counteracted, on the other. The honoring of this aura is best expressed through a responsible compassionate joining, thereby being directed toward the embracing of the client and to the development of closeness. The counteraction is best expressed in an equal co-creation of the culture of embeddedness as well as a deep empowerment of the subjectivity of the client toward self-determination. At the base of this interchange, however, is the inescapable and quasi-autonomic attribution of power to the Spiritual Leader that the care seeker will most likely bring forward. As such, Spiritual Leaders have no choice: they *must* learn to exist within, be comfortable with, and responsibly manipulate authority, power, and charge. Hence, I believe that it is a well-known and often under-appreciated fact that one of the main functions of Spiritual Leaders is to constructively and non-arbitrarily set limits (both prohibitive and permissive) and then, to usefully cultivate those boundaries in the service of the client's Emergence, until it is deemed that the client no longer requires the boundaries for his or her current state of spiritual well-being.

As such, the second function of the Spiritual Leader in the creation of the culture of embeddedness is the promotion of contradictory stimuli that constructively challenge the client's current and particular meaning-making, thereby enhancing and furthering the already begun process of transformation. Thus, the Spiritual Leader is setting limits and promoting the differentiation of the client's consciousness by gradually and gently nurturing an environment in which the client must take charge of greater levels of autonomy, self-control, and self-confidence. The primary challenge of the Direction of Contradiction can be boiled down to the same challenge as that voiced by the Direction of Inclusion: do Spiritual Leaders feel more loyalty to the client's present state of development or are they more committed to the motion of the developing Self?

Just as there were personal reasons within the Spiritual Leader for not being fully able to incorporate anxiety (in our discussion of the Direction of Inclusion), there are personal reasons within the Spiritual Leader that could act as hedges against the progression of a healthy Direction of Contradiction. More specifically, when we engage in the

Direction of Contradiction by setting appropriate boundaries (such as gently disallowing a client to forget a salient and pivotal stimulus, or encouraging the client to further introspect through the asking of a particularly probing question), we encourage the care seeker to continue down the road of evolution, and effectively emerge as a different version of his or her Self. It is not uncommon for Spiritual Leaders to have an affective reaction to this process, however. As with the process of meaning-making, the emergence of a particular Self implies the loss of an older Self—an older Self of which the Spiritual Leader may have been very fond. In other words, as the client's subjectivity undergoes its own spiritual qualitative re-definition, the person that has come to be known, and the one that recruited the Spiritual Leader to his or her attention, will dissolve and be subsumed to another subjectivity. Such a realignment of identity can produce feelings of distance and abandonment within the Spiritual Leader, and therefore may be unwittingly defended against, shunned, or discouraged in some of the most crucial moments of the relationship. Conversely, the defense mounted by the Spiritual Leader may take on a more ominous face: in a relationship based on the redefinition of need and identity, the interplay between client and Leader could result in an aggrandized sense of usefulness and accomplishment within the Leader himself or herself. Such a situation is a form of relational seduction—an enticing and self-edifying temptation that is difficult to overcome. As such, it is possible for Spiritual Leaders to find themselves non-consciously defending an old order of consciousness (thereby safeguarding the current state of the relationship) in order to maintain their own sense of personal worth and usefulness.

Therefore, the Spiritual Leader has no choice but to tackle feelings of loss and sadness as he or she lets go of the 'client-as-present-equilibrium' in order to more fully join with and embrace the 'emerging-Self-as-evolution'. This is part and parcel of the Leader's sacred charge. The client's differentiation and growth is limited to the extent that the created culture of embeddedness can host opposition and otherness, to the extent that it can allow the client to Emerge as a 'someone else'.[14] As such, the level to which care seekers are permitted to develop a sense of empowerment and evolutionary desire is proportional to the caregiver's ability, rooted in personal self-awareness, inner strength, and spiritual

---

14. Kegan, *The Evolving Self,* 127.

groundedness, to contradict and let go of that which has come to be loved: the old form of the client and the old relational prizes.[15]

Kegan states that the failure to assist a care seeker in the natural emergence of the Becoming Self can often take the form of a holding that is too firm (such as a cherishing of the present state equilibrium), or of a separation anxiety that is too harshly expressed (such as a protection of the harmony that has arisen between client and care giver).[16] These actions can unfortunately have the effect of further entangling the relationship between client and Spiritual Leader, and thereby additionally miring the client and the counselor in the current meaning equilibrium (thereby allying them in the staunch defense and maintenance of the current order of consciousness). As such, Kegan warns against the vulnerable side of ourselves that can prefer to remain over-connected and protective of our care seekers, because of a personally vested desire to play out one's individual emotional legacy.

In my opinion, this usually non-conscious activity is tantamount to the abandonment of the client, since the very impetus required for growth is unfairly removed from the possible arising stimuli. Thus, in the most crucial of moments, when the client is building the strength, vision, and stamina to make object the complexities that were once subject in his or her spirituality, the Spiritual Leader's unwitting behavior would foster dependency and closeness, rather than differentiation and integration. Through this unfortunate circumstance, the Spiritual Leader would sabotage the opportunity for Emergence laid in front of the client and allow fear and over-connectedness, as well as limited insight, to reign supreme within the culture of embeddedness.

The Direction of Contradiction carries with it a strong caveat, however. Throughout the entire process of Spiritual Leadership, it is my belief that the client must never doubt the Spiritual Leader's presence and commitment to the process of healing. Therefore, the client must have unwavering confidence that the Spiritual Leader is deeply concerned solely with his or her development, and will remain with him or her, without the slightest possibility of abandonment. The next section is an elucidation of this important environmental factor of the therapeutic relationship: the Direction of Presence.

---

15. Please see Erickson, *Identity and Youth in Crisis*, 113.
16. Kegan, *In Over Our Heads*, 128.

The Direction of Presence

Long ago, I met a couple who were celebrating there sixty-fifth wedding anniversary—a momentous achievement that very few of us will ever have the pleasure of celebrating. At this beautiful occasion, surrounded by family and friends, Elmer (the husband) sat very near his wife and every so often lovingly tapped her hand. She seemed to not notice that her hand was being tapped, as she looked around the room, and yet her hand never moved as her old eyes gleamed with an expression of peace. Later, I was sitting next to Elmer and, being a young man thinking about marriage, I thought I would get this successful man's wise advice. When I asked for the secret of his success, he was offering little but a couple of well-intentioned sarcastic quips, when his son, who had joined our conversation, offered up stories of extreme adversity and difficulty (from financial to medical emergencies, from personal trial to family feuds) that Elmer and his wife had had to weather over their lives. Stunned by the magnitude of what I had just heard, I asked Elmer how he and his wife had muddled through such challenges. Did they talk nightly? Did they take themselves to counseling? How did their connection continue in the whirlwind of stress and the threat of relational extinction? His answer to me was simple, surprising, and profound. Tapping his wife's hand again, he turned to me and simply said, "We just stayed with each other. There really was no other secret. We just stayed."

This story encapsulates the spirit of what I am calling the Direction of Presence. As care worn individuals undergo transformative experiences and engage in rebalancing their subjective apprehensions, they begin to disengage from what used to be, work to find meaning in the disengagement, and grope for the new meaning structure and subjectivity to which they should direct themselves. This emergent process very often sparks three characteristic spiritually-relevant experiences. First, it is during transitional periods such as these that memory, emotional stamina, and relational impetus can suffer. In the confusion that is transformation, a care seeker can often lose sight of the details of the 'former me' as he or she seeks to find the 'new me'. Second, in seeking the 'new me', the care seeker is often in a state of high anxiety not only at the loss of what was cherished (the old subjectivity) but also at the spiritual uncertainty of discovery that comes with uncovering the 'new me'. And third, this transition period unhinges a subjectivity from its embeddedness in a particular context, thereby threatening to promote strong feelings of isolation, solitude, and unacceptability within the groping consciousness of the care seeker.

It is to address all three of these difficult internal states that Spiritual Leaders are to cultivate the Direction of Presence. In essence, the Direction of Presence is defined as simply being there, in the way being is required. In other words, the Direction of Presence is the pledge a Spiritual Leader makes to be available, to be at the client's disposal, and to take on the roles required during the transitional period to promote eventual Emergence. Unlike the Direction of Inclusion, the Direction of Presence is not an intentional and spoken embracing or encouragement of the care seeker. Unlike the Direction of Contradiction, the Direction of Presence is not a deliberate infusion of transformative stimulus into the care relationship. Rather, the Direction of Presence is the unconditional infusion of the subjectivity of the Spiritual Leader into the present culture of embeddedness, such that the client can use it, in any way necessary, as a foil to his or her transformative needs. As such, the Direction of Presence demands the Spiritual Leader develop patience, internal calm, affective mastery, and a thick, understanding skin.

When Peter came to see me, he was beset by considerable regret. Years ago, when he was still in his twenties, he had been engaged to woman named Dora and had fallen deeply in love with her. Over the course of their courtship, however, both Peter and Dora began feeling the pressure (imposed by their particular phase in life) to move beyond the quasi-dependent university mindset, and to make a start at standing on their own two feet. In response of this pressure, each of them started to cultivate personal autonomy and independence to an extent they had never attempted in the past. As a consequence, they each began to experiment with the boundaries of this new found agency by acting with more license and brazenness than was healthy for their relationship. The result was disastrous: irrecoverable words, broken loyalties, and shattered hearts characterized the culture of embeddedness of their relationship. They broke ties in their late twenties.

The story of Peter and Dora is a very common one. Young adults of university age often struggle with their new found liberty, which often finds a confused and bewildering union with the anxiety of succeeding in life's future endeavors. As such, many young adults find that university and post-university relationships are tumultuous and emotionally taxing, at best. In most cases that I have observed, these relationships come to an end. But Peter's regret was not with the tumult of the courtship only. It was also with its aftermath.

After he and Dora parted ways, Peter began to feel a great sense of recrimination toward her and toward the Self he was exhibiting while in relationship with her. He became convinced that his emotional and spiritual health were enhanced after the break up, and went out of his way to make these opinions clear to Dora. Dora responded by being very hurt by Peter's nonchalance and seeming arrogance, and found herself clambering for his approval and regard—a difficult and painful situation which lasted for about a period of 18 months and which led to their complete cutting of ties.

Peter's recrimination subsided, eventually. He had achieved a certain level of career success and had attained a level of autonomy that caused him to feel more accomplished and settled. Slowly, with the passing of time, his attitude toward Dora softened. No longer was he caught in the jaws of anger. Rather, he started to feel as though he missed her, and began wishing to speak with her and to see her. With that intention, he contacted Dora and, after a few strained moments of conversation, extended a long and heartfelt apology to her—both for his behavior during their formal courtship as well as his aggressive behavior after their break up. Dora seemed appreciative of this effort. When he asked her for an update on her life, Dora told him that she had made some changes in her outlook, had begun a new career, and was working to gain a degree of autonomy and control in her life. Although Peter expressed heartfelt admiration for her efforts, he was surprised to find Dora's attitude toward him more stern and aggressive than he had ever heard it. In fact, he thought that she was nothing short of mean. After several months of this, they lost touch again. It was shortly thereafter that Peter came to see me and expressed his regret.

According to his account, he was regretful of having been too young, too unwise to know how to be in a relationship in a constructive fashion during their formal courtship; he was regretful that he assumed an aggressive posture toward Dora in the months after their break-up; he was regretful that he could not reconnect with her and felt that he deserved her ire and her dismissal; most importantly, he regretted the entire story, because he had recently come to the realization of his ever-present and deep love for Dora—a love that he felt would linger, and a heart-break he felt he would have to continually suffer.

The details of this story, with respect to constructivist-developmental growth and Emergence, are very telling. In their youth, both Peter and Dora toiled as hard as they could to maintain a relationship, and yet did not have the spiritual maturity to nurture one another and foster true friendship. In addition, they had entered a phase in their lives where the vagaries of adult autonomy and financial self-sufficiency were gaining ascendancy in their respective consciousnesses. Hence, as a result of their less-than-optimal treatment of each other, in combination with this inevitable shift in their maturing consciousnesses, they could not forge a lasting partnership from which to relate. As such, the relationship ended, but the maturing process did not. As Peter's spirituality evolved further and he began to glimpse the rewards and possibilities of self-possession and autonomy, his former state began to appear untenable to him—as with all experiences of cognitive Piagetian accommodation, once the new equilibrium can be conceived, there is no longer a possibility of backsliding into a former consciousness. In addition to the cognitive, a sense of deep recrimination (against the past stage and/or Self) arises in the emotions, acting as a sort of psychic wall preventing the desire for backsliding at deeper and often unseen levels. Therefore, as we Emerge from one order of consciousness and move into another, we mount a personal defense within our faculties of apprehension which disallows our return to former, and now known to be less mature, states.

In Peter's case, this recrimination arose in his post-courtship attitude toward Dora. As he worked to establish himself and gain stability in his new consciousness, he distanced himself from the younger Self he trying not to be. Dora became a symbol for Peter of that earlier period in his life, and therefore unwittingly became the target of his recriminatory feelings. Thus, it was no coincidence that Peter's aggressiveness toward Dora subsided at just the moment when he felt settled in his new world view. In his new order of consciousness, from this new Self that had made the old Self object to its new subjectivity, not only could Peter clearly see the effects of his behavior while courting Dora, but also the unfairness he exhibited in his attitude towards her after their break-up. In addition to the remorse and shame he began to feel, he was able to perceive the feelings of tenderness he still harbored for Dora deep in his heart. As such, he contacted her and tried to set the records straight. Of course, at this point in her development, Dora was engaged in her own re-equilibration and was using Peter as a symbol of that against which to defend, a symbol of the 'not-me' to which she did not want to return.

With respect to our discussion of the Direction of Presence, the conclusion of this story is illustrative: Peter was coming to terms with the 'Me' that he used to be and is affirming himself as the 'new me'. In so doing, he required me to sit with him and be a witness to the story of his courtship with Dora, to validate him in his struggle to come to terms with his rejected behavior, and literally to see him as he was now trying to be. In so doing, I was able to provide him with a mirror for his memories that his own countenance could not muster, or was unwilling to reflect on in isolation. In addition, as he fought with recurring bouts of anger at his tale, I could act as the diffuser of that anger (on the one hand) when Peter needed calmness, and as the object and repository of that anger (on the other) when he needed to attack and gain some distance from his conceptions. And finally, I simply acted as his companion, as a positive presence in his struggle—a presence that was permissive of his affective swings, his cognitive confusions, and his spiritual dilemmas. In the words of Elmer, I just stayed. As such, by remaining present and consistent in my relationship with Peter, I was able to contribute to our building of a culture of embeddedness that acted as a steadying force, that reminded him of the past Self he was trying to objectify, that provided stability and reliability in his otherwise transforming consciousness, and that reassured him that he was not alone as he struggled with his own sense of shame and doubt. Therefore, the Direction of Presence acts as the very glue that binds together the integration of the Direction of Inclusion and the differentiation of the Direction of Contradiction.

And yet, just as personal affective realities could sabotage Spiritual Leaders as they seek to Include and Contradict, so can they encourage Spiritual Leaders to stray in their pursuit of Presence. In my experience, Spiritual Leaders often feel anxiety at the whirling emotions and recriminations that arise within the client at this crucial juncture. Memories of emotional intensity from the Spiritual Leader's Historical Space will inevitably bring forward protective responses to affective and relational situations thereby potentially moving the Leader into a distancing stance. In other words, in their natural desire to reduce these negative emotions, they may give into the temptation to distance themselves from the relationship, in order to pull away to what they perceive as a safer and self-preserving distance. In addition, this 'pulling away' often comes to be expressed through the Leader's non-conscious avenues, literally resulting in unnoticed, unseen, and un-owned behavior. As Malone and Malone said, "We cannot be responsible for that which we cannot see."[17] In other words, the Leader's subjectivity can itself be fused with these feelings of protection, thereby resulting in autonomic and inscrutable action.

Such a stance of personal defense is fundamentally harmful to the therapeutic relationship as well as to the culture of embeddedness the client needs in order to Emerge. As clients approach the precipice of transformation, internal responses and alarms will become heightened. As such, the closer a client is to the tipping point of Emergence, to more affectively intense the relationship with the Spiritual Leader will likely become. It would therefore be at this crucial juncture of growth that the Leader would pull away, thereby literally abandoning the client just prior to the moment of resurrection. Such abandonment would promote a sense of spiritual confusion, of progressive doubt, and of the need to find a secure grounding. Essentially, pulling away from the client at this critical moment provides the impetus the client may need to retreat to the known (the old subjectivity), to back away from the precipice (to repudiate change), or worse yet, to leap with a sense of deep loneliness and solitude. Such a leap would be tantamount to confirming the client's fears that good faith may not exist in the world (fears already fueled by the fires of transformation), and that transformations end in hard landings. As such, our hapless Spiritual Leader may very well have watched a spiritual crisis end, and caused another to begin.

As with the Directions of Inclusion and Contradiction, a practiced and balanced sense of Self as well as a grounded knowledge of one's affective and relational capabilities is crucial for Spiritual Leaders to avoid such critical and damning pitfalls in the creation of the culture of embeddedness. Making ourselves present to another, literally presenting ourselves for their use in times of movement, can bring forward spiritual challenges of its own—challenges that must be named and overcome by Spiritual Leaders, should they wish their therapeutic interventions to have constructive effects. It is beyond the scope of this work to suggest strategies to build internal spiritual stamina in Spiritual Leaders, yet it is my hope that sounding this urgent bell will further foster interest in just such practices.

---

17. Malone and Malone, *The Windows of Experience*, 91.

In summary, the role of Spiritual Leaders never to abandon or distance themselves from their clients is an overriding requirement for a healthy Emergence from one culture of embeddedness to another more developed and more integrated one. By remaining firmly in place, Spiritual Leaders non-arbitrarily protect the client's opportunities for growth by positioning themselves in the roles required for the transition of the client's consciousness to a new equilibrium. Furthermore, by simply holding a presence within the evolving culture of embeddedness, Spiritual Leaders ensure that the clients' need for innocence and good faith in the world (as the larger context) is advanced and validated. In my opinion, herein lies the basis for the further belief in and development of a deeper spirituality.

6

Creating a Proper Attitude

ATTITUDE WITHIN THE CULTURE OF EMBEDDEDNESS

IN THE LAST FEW chapters, we discussed very important elements in the creation of a culture of embeddedness. These chapters, however, discuss elements that are external to the Spiritual Leader. In other words, neither the goals of the therapeutic relationship nor the environment necessary for evolution are processes that are meant to work on the internal state and therapeutic orientation of the Spiritual Leader. As such, the following section discusses elements in the co-creation of the culture of embeddedness that are internal dispositions held by the constructivist-developmental Spiritual Leader in the creation of the culture of embeddedness. The two topics of relevance to our discussion will be client-centeredness and the art of counter-transference.

Client-Centeredness

George Eliot once said: "The difficult task of knowing another soul is not for young gentlemen whose consciousness is chiefly made up of their own wishes."[1] To paraphrase this thinker, only to the extent that an interpreter/listener recognizes and comprehends the reasons that allow the speaker's observations to appear rational, true, and reasonable to that particular speaker, does he or she begin to understand what the speaker could mean. Therefore, to truly assert that we understand an Other requires the ability to comprehend the order of consciousness of the client, explain the effect of stimuli on his or her spirituality in such a way as the client expresses whole-hearted agreement, to draw links in

---

1. Eliot, *Middlemarch*, 55.

internal arguments in the same way the client would, and to have the ability to draw conclusions from premises in the same way as the client. As such, we are discussing a virtual infusion of the client's subjectivity into that of the Leader, a practical mastery of the client's rules for life engagement. As such, this practice is not the ability to impose a framework on an Other, but rather it is the ability to organize the world as the Other organizes it. Hence, the Spiritual Leader's main orientation is that which focuses him or her on internalizing the meaning-making conventions of the client.

Spiritual Leaders, along with other healers and care-givers, have a dual and concurrent involvement with spirituality, in general, and meaning-making, in particular. They toil tirelessly at joining with their clients within the vagaries of the clients' spiritual systems. Such joining is paramount to Spiritual Leaders' ability to understand the world as clients understand it, and is therefore foundational to a therapeutic interaction. And yet the story for the Leaders is more complex. Whereas clients can focus exclusively on the expression and elucidation of their unique underlying meaning permutations, Spiritual Leaders, already helping clients in this endeavor through attuned joining, must simultaneously take stock, categorize, and otherwise appropriately bracket their own spiritual and meaning-making processes. I believe that it is through the willful and innocent management of these coordinated dual processes of spirituality within the therapeutic relationship that Spiritual Leaders offer a constructive counterpoint to their clients in the creation of an effective culture of embeddedness. As such, when Spiritual Leaders have a seasoned ability to hold their own and their clients' meaning constructions as separate and interdependent entities, I call them attuned helpers. When Spiritual Leaders have a clear idea on how to walk with, nurture, and foster transforming clients as they cope with spiritual upheaval, I call them empathic counselors. When Spiritual Leaders understand how to protect and bring forward stimuli within the therapeutic relationship that promote meaning transformation and Emergence, I call them congruent educators. And, when Spiritual Leaders recognize and develop the appropriate presence they require in order to incarnate the caring required for relational maturity, I call them leaders on the path to Holiness. I can think of no better orientation through which Spiritual Leaders can master these wonderful titles than the client-centered approach.

In order to masterfully pursue the client-centered approach, we must first have an understanding of who our clients are. In my opinion, clients are the builders of their respective worlds and the concretization of their unique Historical Spaces. They are the architects of spirituality and not the made-meaning. They are the evolving spirit and movement of consciousness. They are the masters, the servants, the parents, and the children of their uniquely constructed worlds. They are the Spirit's ever-progressive thrust toward development, maturity, and Holiness. They are the innocent, striving souls who are doing the very best that they can with the resources they have allowed themselves. They are reflections of all the people we have come to love, come to fear, come to emulate, and come to avoid. To the Spiritual Leader, they are foreign entities and familiar faces, objective sources and subjective mirrors. As such, the view from the constructivist-developmental approach is indeed a delicate matter. Its delicacy lies in the fact that the Spiritual Leader is attempting to join with the client in a very intimate way: the Leader is trying to become an integral part of the client's very evolution. Thus, I believe that it is the Spiritual Leader's sacred responsibility to ensure that his or her focus lies entirely within the internal context of the client's constructed meaning-making. Responsible Spiritual Leaders understand that it takes much more than merely a good explanation or rationalization to have clients transform and evolve from their well-defended equilibria. They understand that mere instruction-giving is tantamount to distracting the client from the true work of evolution. Consequently, they develop the instinct to no longer instruct clients, but rather to walk with them empathically as the clients discover new meaning and emerge more evolved Selves.

The Spiritual Leader's attitude, then, is to act as a resonator and mirror to clients, within the clients' meaning organization, in the construction of the culture of embeddedness, in order to compassionately accompany them through the delicate and difficult process of evolution and re-equilibration. In constructivist-developmental terms, this is the essence of the client-centered response.

The client-centered response was passionately championed by Carl Rogers, a therapist who reportedly was notorious for his refusal to answer his clients' questions. His refusal was not in any way malicious, but was based on a concern for the growth and well-being of those he was helping: he believed that his first responsibility was to persuade his clients to find their own answers. He was particularly concerned with ensuring that his presence not promote a relationship in which the clients come to be dependent on him for any reason. As such, he sought to guide them to a place of differentiation and individuality.[2] Therefore, Rogers' hope for his clients betrayed a clear bias, as far as his construction of the form of a healthy person is concerned. Seen from an extra-theory point of view, Rogers wanted his client to place himself or herself at the center of life's evaluative endeavors. He insisted on acting as nothing other than a mirror to his clients' perceptions, thereby offering each of them their own impressions and reactions for further scrutiny. In essence, he wanted each client to be the judge of his or her experience, to be the overseer of his or her motivation, and to be the personal appraiser of value, construction, and evolution. Yet, although Rogers' approach showed great respect for the power and autonomy of the client, it did little to address the contextual issues and relations that inevitably form the cultural aspects of the meaning-making process. In the language of constructivist-developmentalism, therefore, Rogers hoped very strongly for the furtherance of a particular type of spirituality, highly weighted toward the development of differentiation, often at the expense of integration.

In his promotion of personal differentiation and autonomy, and in his refusal to assume an authoritative stance in his therapeutic relationships, Rogers was not open to many roles clients may request or require him to take. As such, he effectively distanced himself from his clients' core sensibilities (a clear turning away from the Direction of Presence). The irony is that in the very instance of his defending the clients' rights to their own meaning-making, Rogers may have effectively been refusing to support that same meaning-making by his unwillingness to take on the transitional roles the clients need him to take on. Thus, the culture of embeddedness would not have been co-created by both partners equally—an imbalance of power that can introduce current-state defense and intimidation into the care-giving relationship. An unequally developed culture of embeddedness is of limited use in the evolution of an innocently striving client, since it does not reflect the complexities and agencies of both members of the relationship. It is therefore essentially an artificial relational construct that risks promoting artificial intervention and relation. Recall that only in the fullness of an experienced relation,

2. For more on this, please see Rogers, *Client-Centered Therapy*.

only in the totality of the subject-object relationship, can insight bolster our attempts at transformation. In agreement with Kegan, I believe that such therapy, despite its strengths and deep compassion, often counsels at a level that is outside the order of consciousness of the client, thereby leaving the client frustrated and confused, with a much longer road to transformation and evolution.[3]

In its deep belief in transformation and evolution, the constructivist-developmental client-centered response differs from the famous Rogerian response with regards to his two seminal assertions. First, in disagreement with Rogers' sole practice of furthering a differentiated order of consciousness within his clients, constructivist-developmentalism stipulates a deep sensitivity and awareness of the requirements and limitations of all the other developmental stages. According to the constructivist-developmental conception of client-centeredness, the responsible Spiritual Leader should first be able to assess the clients' construction of spirituality and second, be able to provide them with the culture of embeddedness they truly need in order to join intimately with the Leader. After the joining has successfully solidified, the Spiritual Leader can do his or her part in the relationship to create a culture of embeddedness that promotes the evolution of consciousness and Emergence.[4] The crux of this theory is found in the refusal to assume a particular order of consciousness, or to presume a particular level of functioning on the part of the client. I believe that it is only in accepting, sincere, and relevant twinning, that clients and Leaders can move forward in the processes of healing and evolution.[5]

In disagreement with the second seminal Rogerian assertion, constructivist-developmentalism is not solely focused on the differentiation of clients. It states that a responsible Spiritual Leader is just as concerned with forces of differentiation as he or she is with forces of integration. Although the Rogerian conception fosters a strong sense of autonomy and personal identity, it does not go so far as to also actively and vocally promote the healthy integration of the differentiated self into the newly perceived subject-object balance. Constructivist-developmentalism

---

3. Kegan, *In Over Our Heads*, 246.

4. As such, this is highlighting the contextual direction of promoting self-determination, encouraging insight, and protecting growth opportunities—three of the hallmark goals of Spiritual Leadership.

5. For more on twinning, see Kohut, *The Analysis of Self*.

does not believe that autonomy is the final ground of psychological health. Rather, the theory stipulates that psychological health is inseparable from philosophical and spiritual health. Therefore, the very functions of an integrated socialization and internalized retrospection are paramount to the fullest expression of a complete Self. It is not enough to simply grow into ourselves. It is crucial that we also internalize the complexities of the world into ourselves, and ourselves into the complexities of the world. As such, we emulate the example of the Divine 'I', who is both fully differentiated and fully integrated.

The client-centered orientation is an extremely powerful and demanding practice that requires great presence, congruence, and attunement from the Spiritual Leader. Throughout the constructivist-developmental interpretation of this approach, the Leader must not seek to or decline to take on any roles (including that of diagnostician, when appropriate) required by the client (within the boundaries of professional ethics, of course). The Leader only seeks to be present and to non-arbitrarily protect the growth opportunities for the client. The Leader co-creates the culture of embeddedness and holds the proverbial door open, while actively resonating with the organized world of the client. In so doing, he or she turns away from the seductive temptation to solve the clients' problems or to try to make the entire process less painful. The Spiritual Leader, then, prizes the client as the 'Self who makes meaning' and not as the 'person as *fait accompli*'. In my opinion, when properly practiced, the constructivist-developmental approach to the client-centered orientation is one of the clearest manifestations of Christ-like love.

It cannot be overstressed, however, that despite the effort to remain client-centered, the Spiritual Leader must have certain preferences and attitudes that are entirely his or her own. This is a natural and expected by-product of the simple fact that Spiritual Leaders are themselves human travelers on the road of evolution. I believe that it is important to discuss this complex element of the therapeutic relationship. As such, the next section discusses the art of counter-transference. This artful practice involves the combined elements of the Spiritual Leader using his or her reactions as therapeutic information, on the one hand, and of bracketing these very motivations in order to walk solely with the client's agenda, on the other.

Counter-Transference

Kant once wrote: "We can only conceive of another subject by imputing our own subjectness to another entity."[6] On the surface, this assertion sounds like the very opposite of the client-centered approach we discussed in the last section. But what Kant meant is much more mundane and practical then our relational aspirations. He believed that to develop viable ways of being in the world, each person must learn to make predictions about the objects he or she constructs. These predictions, when left unattended, often take the form of an infusion of the Other's consciousness with our own, thereby resulting in a homogeneous and self-constructed view of the world. In other words, we cannot help but to default to generating explanations of how Others function on the basis of our subjective experiences. Therefore, in the office of every Spiritual Leader, there are ghosts: these are the shades of the Leaders past, the complexities of his or her present, and the dreams of his or her future. Together, they compose the monolithic structure that is the Spiritual Leader's construction of Self and reality. These constructions, and their influences upon the client's actions and presented stimuli, are generally referred to as Counter-Transference. Although counter-transference is a vital component of the culture of embeddedness, it is at the same time, a potential hurdle that limits the Leader's vision of the client as he or she truly is. In other words, the Leader's constructed reality can, if left unchecked, go so far as to also construct the very client in his or her meaning-making—the very opposite of the exigencies of client-centeredness. This danger carries ramifications for the perception of the conscious preferences the client makes, and as such can present itself as a fundamental stumbling block to intimate joining. For example, a Spiritual Leader who demonstrates the capacity to reflect on, rather than be driven by, feelings may lose sight of the fact that his or her client might not be constructing reality in the same manner. As such, the client may not exhibit similar reactions to the Spiritual Leader when confronted with the same compelling stimulus. Thus, attending to the feelings that arise in me (as the Spiritual Leader) may give insight into the culture of embeddedness and the manner in which the client makes meaning, but can never be used as a benchmark through which to determine how a client puts his or her world together. Consequently, if the client does not

---

6. Kant in Steffe and Gale, *Constructivism in Education*, 12.

exhibit the same emotions I am feeling, it does not automatically imply, as a great number of unfortunate Leaders immediately assume, that the client is in some type of denial. As such, the Spiritual Leader's main attitude in regards to his or her emotions is to use them as a guidepost to understand the culture of embeddedness, and then to bracket them in order to more fully see the client.

Bracketing is a considered and practiced activity that involves a Spiritual Leader's emotional and willful control. Through this process, Leaders intentionally put their emotional constructions and preferences aside in order to forge an intimate connection with the client, unimpeded by the vagaries of personal bias. It is a function of discipline because, as an art form in itself, it requires time, practice and perfection. It is a function of responsibility because it requires ownership, confidence, and a balanced response to the intricacies of the clients meaning-making. And, it is a function of spirit because it creates the circumstances through which a Leader can perceive the total acceptability and beauty of the client as a child of God.[7] Bracketing, then, is a fundamental component of Spiritual Leadership that under girds the ability of Leaders to foster the Direction of Inclusion because it accepts and acclaims the client as he or she truly is. It is a fundamental component of the Direction of Contradiction because it allows the Spiritual Leader to act outside the lens of personal preference and experience, and thereby challenge the client in the unique way, and at the unique construction of consciousness, that is most useful to healing and growth. And, it is a fundamental component of the Direction of Presence because Leaders can more effectively and efficiently forge the intimate connection required to provide presence and support as the client emerges from one culture of embeddedness and integrates into a new one.

As with all components of Spiritual Leadership, however, the practice of controlling counter-transference is a dialectical one. Although the discussion so far has focused on the bracketing of emotions and preferences, it is in no way to be interpreted as a call for the elimination of the Spiritual Leader's emotional and preferential sides altogether. In classic dialectical fashion, the presence of the Leader's emotional and preferential drives is crucial to the success of a healing relationship. How so?

When Freud developed his psychoanalytic theory, he simultaneously developed two main tenets of connection. In his first tenet, he stated that

7. For more on bracketing, please see Peck, *The Road Less Traveled*, 34.

a healing relationship with another could be successful only if client and Helper engage in a fully motivated partnership, and a sincere contract of pursuing growth. His second tenet was particularly relevant to counter-transference: he believed that a Helper will not perceive in the client what he or she has not learned to recognize in their own Self.[8] Therefore, a Spiritual Leader must divide himself or herself into two parts: the observer and the observed. A Spiritual Leader has to relinquish the safety of the authoritarian 'expert' role, the all-knowing parental figure that carries all the answers in a magic storehouse of information. By observing his or her own emotions and preferences throughout the personal and professional development that has led the Leader to this place in history, he or she names, understands, makes object, and works to overcome the very difficult forces that are now arising for the troubled client. Thus, the Leader and the client stand together as fellow human travelers on God's path, each striving for a higher conception of meaning-making that renders the world more orderly, more loving, more holy. Consequently, the strings of the Spiritual Leader's motivations will be pulled, sometimes consciously and sometimes non-consciously, by the sheer fact that he or she is in a relationship with a client, who is both object and mirror. The Leader will not be able, for long, to escape the necessary conflict between his or her emotional participation in the observed events, and the methodological rigor required to impute counter-transference into the creation of a culture of embeddedness which encourages the advancement of the client's evolution. Therefore, the Spiritual Leader's great discipline is an act of piety in which the Leader learns to develop the ability to integrate the observational field of the relationship, with the methodological responsibilities of Leadership, with the human obligations of respect, attunement, and love. This orientation, in my opinion, stands as the basis from which the Leader engages in and wrestles with the inescapable conflict between the rational aims of the observed and the self-preserving fixations of the observer, where observer and observed are *both* internal and external. Stated in this fashion, this orientation of piety no longer limits itself to the professional field. As such, it spreads its wings of influence and touches the motivations underlying all relationships in the Spiritual Leader's life.

Hence, to paraphrase Erickson, it is the mark of responsible and adept Spiritual Leaders that much can go on within them without clog-

---

8. E. Erickson, *Childhood and Society,* 147, and Freud, *Basic Writings,* 68–73.

ging their communications within the moments of the healing relationship. Aware, yet emptied of professional dogmatism and stringent orthodox adherence to their Historical Spaces, Spiritual Leaders carry with them an implicit insight and specific style of action.[9] This style of action creates a culture of embeddedness, geared entirely toward the client's center, non-arbitrarily protecting the opportunities that arise and leading the client to new choices, self-determination, insight, and new consciousness. To my mind, it is a mighty driven-ness, an intense and flexible energy, a spiritual innovation, a responsible loving-kindness, and a fundamentally moral and beautiful orientation toward the development of Holiness. And none of these powerful elements would be possible without the responsible and considered manipulation of counter-transference.

---

9. Coles, *The Erik Erickson Reader*, 183.

7

Constructivist-Developmental Practices

THE APPLICATION OF CONSTRUCTIVIST-DEVELOPMENTAL METHODS: THE CPSS MODEL

BEFORE TURNING MY ATTENTION more fully to some activities of constructivist-developmental Leadership, I think it would be beneficial to summarize the major topics we have covered, which are of direct relevance to the practice of constructivist-developmental Leadership techniques.

1. Constructivist-developmentalism is theory of consciousness which holds several principles as essential: a) knowledge is not passively received but is actively interpreted and integrated by the client; b) meaning is actively built up by the evolving Subject; c) the function of equilibration is adaptive and tends toward viability; and d) thought and emotion serve the client's immediate experiential world. These are the conceptual foundations on which Spiritual Leaders can have confidence in the judgment and agency of each client in the process of his or her development and growth.

2. Constructivist-developmentalism holds several tenets as true: a) we are not made up by the experience of an Other, b) the Other is not made up by his or her experience, c) we are not made up of our own experience, d) the Other is not made up by our experience. These are the conceptual foundations which protect constructivist-developmental practitioners from taking on responsibilities that are not their own, as well as unwittingly assigning to their clients responsibilities which do not belong to them.[1]

---

1. Lonergan, *Insight*, 6; Kegan, *In Over our Heads*, 128.

3. Constructivist-developmentalism makes the following assumptions about clients engaged in real life events: a) clients conceive individually to make personal meaning out of events; b) clients think collaboratively within their culture to make shared meanings of particular events; c) clients connect their prior experience and current order of consciousness to the current evolutionary challenge; d) clients actively question themselves and their culture to help reconcile the challenges inherent in growth stimulating events; e) clients can present their conceptions of the therapeutic relationship in many different ways; and f) clients can reflect currently and retroactively on the complexities and processes of a particular transformation event.

These are all the conceptual foundations that can be used to inform the Context-Phase-Stage-Style (CPSS) model of Leadership, proposed by Karen Eriksen.[2] The elucidation of this model is the purpose of this final section. In my discussion of this model, I will be following Eriksen's lead. I will, however, be modulating its presentation in order to better incorporate elements of the Spiritual Leadership context, as well as the tenets of our foregoing discussion.

In light of the above summaries and in the wake of the many exigencies required of the Spiritual Leader while in relationship with a client, several interrelational implications arise as the foundations of the CPSS model. It is worth summarizing these implications for clarity:

1) The Spiritual Leader must carry a deep respect for, and a knowledge of how to walk with the client through the complex maze of the client's order of consciousness (Direction of Inclusion);

2) Psycho-educational practices which encourage the client to remedy challenges are an integral component of the Spiritual Leadership relationship (Direction of Contradiction);

3) The client engages in a super-rational and meta-phenomenological self-regulation throughout the process of transformation (development of Selfhood);

4) Spiritual Leaders are called upon to engage in the creative representations of concepts and challenges in order to facilitate client spirituality and evolution (non-arbitrary protection of opportunities);

2. Eriksen, "Constructivist and Developmental Identity".

5) Spiritual Leaders must always hold in the forefront of their minds the goals of the client as well as the differences between the client's goals and the Leader's preferred outcome (the art of counter-transference);

6) Spiritual Leaders and clients must incorporate the complexities and vagaries of the client's social context, including inherited mottos, myths, and folk logic, into the relationship (Historical Space);

7) Spiritual Leaders must remain circumspect and reflexive, resisting the tendency to associate a single path with absolute truth (vagaries of meaning-making);

8) The concern of Spiritual Leaders is not just the clients' knowledge, but most importantly his or her spiritual development (insight and self-determination);

9) The Spiritual Leader's knowledge of subject matter and diagnostic skills is not as important as his or her convicted belief in the personal theory of human consciousness evolution (client-centeredness);

10) The Spiritual Leader is called upon to recognize and honor areas of strength as well as elements of limitation within the clients constructions (tenets of constructivism and developmentalism).

With the foregoing summaries in mind, I turn my attention to the CPSS model of engagement.

The CPSS Model

The CPSS model is a platform upon which Spiritual Leaders can approach their clients. It is a model that is most useful in the joining and discovery phases of the Leadership relationship and is a very useful tool in helping Leaders make constructivist-developmental determinations about their presenting clients. The model itself is focused on individual clients (rather than on generalized therapeutic tenets) and goes a long way to promoting intra-therapeutic self-reflection, spiritual awareness, and cultural attunement.[3] As such, the practices in the CPSS model are strongly wellness-oriented and culturally sensitive interventions. They are questioning techniques that provide the required information that can serve as the substrates for more advanced therapeutic interven-

3. Eriksen, "Constructivist and Developmental Identity".

tions. It is a model, based on constructivist-developmental tenets, that is meant to glean relevant information from the client in order to build a better suited and customized culture of embeddedness through which the client can transform. It is comprised of four main components: social Context, life Phase, constructive Stage, and personality Style. These four components are perceptual lenses through which to view the relationship, so as to promote the ability to maximize positive inclinations and accumulated strengths, bringing these powerful attributes to the process of the client's transformation and Emergence. The model can also provide Spiritual Leaders with a framework for applying the various complexities of the constructivist-developmental growth theory, the interpersonally driven process of co-creating the culture of embeddedness, the intra-personally oriented practices of client-centeredness and controlled counter-transference, and the intuitive, inspired insights which found the basis through which the Leader can intimately join and connect to the client. I will discuss each of the elements of this model separately.

CONTEXT

As we saw in our discussion of Historical Space, the constructivist-developmental growth theory believes that human consciousness is inextricably linked to the cultural and social surround in which it is evolving. As such, a person's reality, thoughts, facts, emotions, preferences, and so on, are intrinsically culture-influenced and community-maintained internal entities. From this perspective, the social dimension of experience is so pervasive that no person, at any given time, can be separated from his or her past social experiences or present cultural influences. According to Gagnon, even when we are alone, our very consciousnesses and meanings are bound up in the languages and conventions, social categories and cultural values of our contexts.[4] Through this dimension of approach, Spiritual Leaders and clients are asked to look through the specific lenses of family, community, faith, and cultural surround in order to better understand the elements of the construction of meaning of the clients. To this end, Karen Eriksen highlights the eight specific social identities of gender, ability, race, religion, ethnicity, age, class, and sexual orientation, and suggests that each permutation of identity carries with it a cumulative layer of meaning influence within the contextualized

4. Gagnon and Collay, *Designing for Learning*, 256.

client.[5] Awareness of the Spiritual Leader to these facets of social existence, in conjunction with those of Historical Space, sensitizes him or her to the dual issues of internalized client assumptions based on these contexts, as well as external issues of power, aggrandizement, or oppression through which clients must struggle. It is to all these elements that Spiritual Leaders must attend as they assess the client's social context.

Context assessment is essentially the Spiritual Leader's practice of considering the impact of the client's social surround, social identities, internalized assumptions, Historical Space, and externalized defenses on the present constructive meaning-making of the client, as well as the practice of negotiating how these elements are best accessed to protect opportunities for growth and facilitate transformation. The best tool at the Spiritual Leader's disposal for this type of assessment is empathic questioning. The constructivist-developmental framework for posing questions and accessing information can be summarized by the Explore-Perceive-Act approach.[6] In the first instance, the Spiritual Leader is challenged to explore the situational, family, community, and cultural contexts in which the client developed and in which the client currently exists. In so doing, the Leader will be able to gather necessary information that will help him or her understand how best to be client-centered and what the possible effects of counter-transference will be. In addition, the Leader will be better able to glimpse the trajectory of insight that characterizes the client's unique development, and thereby develop a sense of how to foster self-determination. In the second instance, the Spiritual Leader is challenged to Perceive the implicit, socially derived assumptions that are embedded in the social constructions of the client. In so doing, the Leader can develop a firm apprehension of the shape of the client's underlying meaning structure and subjective self-definition—the main reagents in the transformative reaction. And in the third instance, the Spiritual Leader is challenged to Act in the relationship in order to better foster growth, connection, and transformation. Kegan warned about the difference between being the protector of opportunities for growth (a position he promoted) and being the creator of opportunities, the originator of stimuli, and the

---

5. Eriksen, "Constructivist and Developmental Identity", 5.

6. I am here taking some license with Eriksen's model, modulating it to better fit a spiritual context. Her original conception is that of Explore-Know-Act. Eriksen, "Constructivist and Developmental Identity", 6.

directive driver of evolution.[7] I agree with his assessment that placing oneself as the creator of opportunities is a form of therapeutic arrogance that conducts the healing relationship on the terms of the Leader, rather than through the needs of the care seeker. As such, by better fostering connection and awareness, the Perceive phase of the intervention model works to counteract this dangerous eventuality and guide the impetus of the Act phase. In addition, in this context, the word 'Act' can mean everything from accepting, to contradicting, to remaining present.

Although an entire volume could be written on the art of questioning, I believe that discussion to be beyond the scope of this particular work. I will simply follow Karen Eriksen's example and provide a sample framework of questions for assessing a client's social context. Since constructivist-developmentalism is focused on the underlying meaning-making of the client, all questions posed are open-ended and are meant to encourage the client to truly investigate the hidden influences in which he or she has constructed reality. Some questions that are well geared to assessing context are the following:

- What did your family's social class mean to you?
- What do your family's messages regarding success mean to you?
- What do you think of your family's attitude toward. . . ?
- What role did religious faith play in your conception of goodness?
- How do you experience your role in your current family?
- What does that fairy tale mean to you?
- What does God look like for you?
- What's it like for you, to be Italian?
- What have you enjoyed most/least about being a woman?
- What was that tragic event like for you?
- What made Mr. Smith so influential for you at that time? What do you think of him today, looking back?
- What kind of person would you go to today if you needed support?

---

7. Kegan, *Evolving Self*, 283.

I agree with many sociological and constructivist-developmental scholars that many clients are not aware of the degree to which social contexts have affected them. The reason for this gap in awareness is the counter-intuitive inclination of its ramifications in our Western, individualistic culture. To help counter-balance this person-oriented bias, I believe that Spiritual Leaders are called upon to be intimately aware of the continuing influences of their own Historical Spaces, the very mechanics of their counter-transferences. As such, they will be more attuned to social and cultural discourse, and therefore be able to more easily recognize complexities in the lives of their clients and be more useful in the protection of opportunities for growth. Consequently, context-oriented interventions encourage the Spiritual Leader to be present for the client in two distinct ways: first, they help the client objectify, name, categorize, understand, and rewrite the social narratives that prove themselves to be foundational in their lives; and second, Leaders can use the contextual information to help their clients transform their consciousness of the importance of the social component, and thereby encourage them to mine the positive and action-producing power of these same contexts.

PHASE

As I mentioned earlier in the section on Historical Space, a phase can be defined as a psychosocial construction which refers to an interval of time in the lifespan of a person during which certain themes, such as education, career development, or family formation, are ascendant.[8] Erik Erikson's seminal work in the development of psychosocial stages throughout the lifecycle made it clear that appropriate phase navigation is paramount to emotional and relational health as well as to the furtherance of subsequent development. In fact, his scheme is predicated on the notion that psychosocial development is cumulative, rather than successive. In other words, a person's conquering of the psychosocial challenges of a particular phase is the pre-requisite for his or her ability to move and tackle the challenges at the next psychosocial stage.[9] As such, phase considerations form the basis of successful evolution from one psychosocial stage to a more generative one.

---

8. Eriksen, "Constructivist and Developmental Identity", 7.
9. Coles, *The Erik Erickson*, 342.

A phase is comprised of two main elements: first, a coalescence of physical, cognitive, and emotional states of readiness to tackle the complexities of the perceived life era on behalf of the subject; and second, a conglomeration of the social expectations made of individuals by the cultural surround, which are generally uniform, and age-specific demands on each member of the culture. Erik Erikson claims that the social expectations of psychosocial stages carry with them a number of implications to growth. They define a developmental crisis as the transition individuals undergo when their behavior and expected mindsets do not match the psychosocial exigencies of the cultural surround. In these cases, the individual is confronted with the frightening prospects of redefining the Self in relation to its context in order to better fulfill the perceived demands.[10] Carl Rogers added his voice to this discourse by pointing out that psychosocial rebalancing does not occur in a single cataclysmic spiritual event. Rather, according to his work, psychosocial rebalancing begins well before the emergence of the presenting crisis, in the guise of transformative challenges of smaller proportion—like warning tremors that might precede a larger earthquake.[11] For example, the crises which challenge adults around the issues of career choice and generativity, will often have been preceded by crises in the choices of meaning in work, volunteer opportunities, and humanitarian investigation.

Thus, if the dominant groups in Western society expect "school-age children to be industrious in their school work, adolescents to begin interacting romantically with one another, adults to teach and mentor the younger generation, and elders to shift their focus toward modified career choices and leisure pursuits", the societal and popular conception of individual health will likely revolve around the achievement of these phases at the right time in development.[12] Aberrations of this pattern are unfortunately frequently judged as abnormal, eccentric, and even dysfunctional.[13] In addition, Karen Eriksen's eight social identities described above modulate these expectations in often prescribed and predictable ways.[14]

10. Coles, *The Erik Erickson Reader*, 268.
11. Rogers in Gagnon and Collay, *Designing for Learning*, 278.
12. Eriksen, "Constructivist and Developmental Identity", 6.
13. Gagnon and Collay, *Designing for Learning*, 95.
14. The eight social identities are gender, ability, race, religion, ethnicity, age, class, and sexual orientation. For more on this, please see Eriksen, "Constructivist and

Spiritual Leaders and clients are inescapably affected and individually moulded within these psychosocial stages. Even without the formal knowledge of Erik Erikson's stages, it is my belief that both members of the therapeutic relationship are well-imbued with an intuitive knowledge of the complexities and exigencies set forth by the cultural surround in general (provided they are immersed in similar societal biases). It is in its more specific incarnations that psychosocial stages can be elusive to an unaware or inattentive Spiritual Leader. For example, the broad societal expectation that young adults prepare for the challenges of marriage can be concretized in a subset of the population as a stipulation that each member of the subculture will only marry a mate of similar ethnicity. I do not believe that a Spiritual Leader can be aware of the detailed and specific complexities of the subculture in which the client functions, unless investigations and assessments of the client's constructions of life phases and exigencies take place, in relation to the client's context. Here again, we see the importance of understanding Historical Space.

Spiritual Leaders can assess phasic complexities and considerations by questioning the client on issues of engagement in the perceived tasks of their specific life phase.[15] The questions asked must be focused on the most salient features of the ideal life stage:

- Is your career progressing as you would have wished?
- What would it mean to you if you broke up with your girlfriend?
- What is your favorite/least favorite part of going to school?
- Do you think God would want you to decide that on your own?
- What does it mean to you to be pretty?
- Now that you're 60 years old, how do you feel about the career you have led?
- What does it mean to disappointment God?
- At work, what are you doing that is consistent with what you love to do?
- Do you feel you are adequately connected with your spouse?
- Why do you feel it is important to always ask for permission?

Developmental Identity", 6.

15. Eriksen, "Constructivist and Developmental Identity", 7.

- Do you trust God?
- Do you think you are good at that task?
- What does it for you, that you are not currently employed?

This line of questioning is meant to make conscious the phase-appropriate struggles and preoccupations that are confronting the client. It is often the case that clients cannot verbalize the nature of their sense of *dis*-ease, and therefore require the spur of probing questions and a caring eye. As such, from such discourse, questions surrounding trust, will, competence, love, autonomy, generativity, and even wisdom can be marshaled in the defense and protection of the transforming spirit In helping clients become more aware of their societal expectations, Spiritual Leaders can further non-arbitrarily protect and foster opportunities for the client to self-determinedly reconstruct and objectify their responses to these demands. Once objectified and brought into the sphere of the visible, the phase tasks through which the client is struggling can be named and honored by the Spiritual Leader, who can evoke the powers of such practices as intentional reciprocity, insight encouragement, emotionally focused therapy, psychodynamic relationalism and other intervention models, in a compassionate and prayerful fashion. Therefore, clients can come to feel a greater degree of readiness toward upcoming life stage transitions as well as feel normalized in the struggles they undergo. Also, Spiritual Leaders and clients can explore alternative, less conventional methods of achieving satisfaction in life phases, methods that more sincerely and harmoniously fit into the client's current meaning-making. And, in the words of Karen Eriksen, "in the final analysis, such compassionate and loving questionings can encourage the client to de-construct certain rigid interpretations of phasic tasks, interpretations that frequently result in guilt, fear, and low self-regard."[16] Through this sincere interaction, I believe that the client will be more likely to entertain thoughts and options of investigation and progression toward a greater Spiritual health.

STAGE

The foregoing chapters dealt with the meaning, structure, and incarnation of constructivist-developmental spiritual growth. It comes as no surprise that knowledge of the client's stage is a useful tool in the Spiritual

16. Eriksen, "Constructivist and Developmental Identity", 8.

Leadership relationship. Stage theory can be defined as a developmental construct that posits regular, progressive changes in how meaning-making and spirituality evolve over a lifecycle. As I stated earlier, a full elucidation of stage theories is beyond the scope of this particular work. The details of such work, however, can readily be found in the psychotherapeutic literature.[17] A caveat must be stated, however: I believe that Spiritual Leaders must be very careful to nurture, love, and foster the client as the person who evolves and continually makes meaning (as we saw in the sections of the Directions of Inclusion, Contradiction, and Presence). Too often, I have perceived stage theories fall into the hands of practitioners who are more concerned with categorization and the labeling of clients, more interested in diagnosing stage attenuation then in fostering Emergence, more interested in observing from a distance rather than deeply connecting with the client. Knowledge of stages is important relationally, only insofar as it provides the Spiritual Leader with a somewhat understandable set of organizing principles under which the client's spirituality is currently functioning. As such, stages give a hint into the client's epistemology—but it is only a hint. The diversity that can be expressed in stage incarnation is as vast as that seen in Historical Space investigations, and Spiritual Leaders would do well to remain humble in the face of such complexity. It is assumed in stage models, though, that the more flexible, open, complex, and accepting constructive capacities are hallmarks of greater maturity and capacity for self-authored growth.[18]

Stage assessments can be undertaken through a specific type of questioning: questions that are meant to elicit the meanings that are held behind the client's statements and actions. In this way, both the Spiritual Leader and client can have a clearer view of the epistemology within which the client is embedded.

- What struck you as most important in that situation?
- Why are you so scared of losing. . . ?
- What would God say to you if He were here right now?

---

17. For more on stage theory, please see Fowler, *Stages of Faith;* Kegan, *Evolving Self;* Kohlberg, *Moral Stages;* Erikson, *Childhood and Society;* Piaget, *Constructions of Reality;* Perry, *College Years.*

18. Eriksen, "Constructivist and Developmental Identity", 9.

- Why does her opinion of you matter so much?
- What would be the worst thing that could happen as a result of this situation?
- What do you want to have happen with this?
- What does it mean to you to not be liked?
- Why do you believe that about God?
- What is the best way to help you through this?
- What do you need from me right now?

Following an initial response to such questions, clients and Spiritual Leaders can proceed to an investigation of the underlying assumptions that make up the current order of consciousness, to create an internal picture of the meaning-making arrangement that feeds and illuminates current spirituality, thus presenting itself ever-more for objectification. It is also through such questioning that elements of internal authorship (or lack thereof) can be highlighted and attended to within the healing relationship. As such, gaps in differentiation and integration can be further objectified in order to be more diligently worked upon by the emergent subject.

Upon the realization of the identity of the emergent subject, Spiritual Leaders can more effectively join in an intimate fashion and create an appropriate culture of embeddedness by matching the clients in areas of strength and gently mismatching the client in areas of limitation. The resultant culture of embeddedness will create an environment, which holds the client in his or her strengths, contradicts the client in areas of limitation, and remains unwaveringly present with the client throughout the entire process. As such, a proper application of stage knowledge combined with the attitudinal and environmental complexities mentioned earlier will lay a solid groundwork upon which the client can evolve spiritually and learn to be more self-determinative.

Style

I do not believe that a full discussion of personality styles is within the scope of this book. That does not preclude me, however, from stating the important contributions personality styles make to the therapeutic relationship between Spiritual Leaders and clients. Personality styles can be defined as the preferred modes through which an individual is comfortable operating. Therefore, personality styles are the relatively consistent inclinations that individuals display across various contexts.[19] Often, the word personality 'trait' or 'type' is used to name elements of personal preference with regards to conduct and being. To paraphrase Karen Eriksen, scholars often use the more biologically driven notion of 'temperament' in helping their clients know, accept, and manage their particular inclinations and preferences. Such terms as energetic, artistic, even-tempered, extroverted, investigative, compulsive, and reactive are among some very common descriptors of what I am calling personality styles. Much like stage conceptions, however, personality styles should be recognized as constructed approximations of a client's experience, arrayed on a continuum of experiential responses, rather than being reified and totalized in all-or-nothing terms.[20] As such, in agreement with Karen Eriksen, I believe that Spiritual Leaders must take their responsibility to client-centeredness, artful counter-transference, insight, and transformation very seriously in order to ensure that they do not fall into the trap of stereotyping clients as static personalities, phases, or spiritualities. Karen Eriksen points out that 'style' differs from 'stage' in that it represents a long-term constructive preference rather than a current and developing constructive capacity.[21] In other words, whereas stages are transient structures that help us construct and make meaning of our worlds today, styles are quasi-permanent inclinations that allow us to deal with the complexities of the stages within a particular mode of action. Stages and personality styles, however, are similar in their concern with an individual's consistent tendencies over time, whether it be in epistemology (stages) or in preference of action (style).[22]

The ability to perceive connections with stages and phase conceptions, however, carries within it a normalizing tendency that I believe is very constructive. By normalizing tendency, I refer to the notion that, by understanding something about a person's phase and personality style, we can better fit that person's struggles into the greater human story, thereby alleviating concerns of unacceptable loneliness, or neurotic uniqueness. This normalization is of great importance, in my opinion, since culture has a tendency of prizing certain personality features over

19. Eriksen, "Constructivist and Developmental Identity", 10.
20. Steffe and Gale, *Constructivism in Education*, 312.
21. Eriksen, "Constructivist and Developmental Identity", 10.
22. Kegan, *The Evolving Self*, 232.

others, thereby resulting in a mild, yet palpable discrimination against the members of society who exhibit the non-dominant traits. Normalization serves to equalize the playing field thus opening a door to a myriad of options that may not have been readily available to the client before the Spiritual Leadership relationship.

An assessment of personality style is, in my opinion, one of the most intuitive and automatic events within any relationship. Within minutes of meeting a new person, we have usually formulated a conception of that person's style, as well as an opinion regarding the effectiveness of that style. Personality theorists, however, go to great lengths to state that apparent personality traits may not be direct reflections of the true, underlying personality style. Therefore, many style-assessing tools have been created, and have permeated the fields of education and psychology for many decades. The Spiritual Leader, however, can make a reliable assessment of personality style by engaging in a focused and gentle form of questioning:

- What's your perfect workplace and why?
- What kind of people annoy you the most?
- How do energize yourself?
- When you pray, do you easily wander off topic?
- What's your favorite board game?
- What is your preferred way of coming up with new ideas?
- Do you prefer to pray in words and formulas or do you meditate quietly?
- How do you connect with your best friends?
- Do you play a musical instrument? Tell me about that...

Clearly, a sound knowledge of personality theories is required in order for such an assessment to be accurate. As such, it is my belief that, in addition to topics such as psychology, sociology, theology, and Biblical philosophy, Spiritual Leaders must have a firm educational grounding in the complexities and interrelations of personality styles.

The knowledge of the style preferences of clients leads to several important and healing implications. The first is the awareness in the client of his or her own preferences in an objectified manner, a knowledge that can be promoted using the Explore-Perceive-Act model proposed earlier. Through a knowledge of their own styles and an awareness of the common challenges faced by those who share their personality preferences, I believe that clients can begin on a road to inner peace and self-acceptance that forms the very basis of development throughout spiritual growth. In addition, clients can begin to name the very real strengths and assets they carry within them, elements that may have been taken for granted in the past. Once named, once made Object, these strengths can be called upon in a new and intentional fashion that increases the client's stamina and drive for growth and development.[23] In contrast, the objectification of personality styles can go a long way to helping the client foster the non-dominant traits within the Self, which tend to be the traits that are most called upon in times of crisis.[24] Therefore, an intentional objectification and development of non-dominant capacities carries within it the possibility of more effectively and efficiently weathering the storms of future crises, thereby increasing the likelihood and smoothness of meaning development.

A FINAL THOUGHT

The foregoing discussion has outlined a great number of capacities, complexities and talents that I believe Spiritual Leaders are called upon to develop. I believe that these abilities are crucial in guiding and walking with others as they find their unique expression of Spiritual maturity. Since my definition and framework of Spirituality outlined in Section 1 is inclusive of all the other major elements of Being, I believe that it is the role of Spiritual Leaders to be well-educated and well-seasoned in the myriad realms and orders that make up human consciousness. Therefore, Spiritual Leadership is not only one of the most important occupations to my mind, it is also one of the most taxing in terms of preparation, study, and personal maturity. My hope is that this work and the subsequent work that flows from it, will help transform the consciousness of the profession of Spiritual Leadership into a consciousness that understands its role to be so much more vast than the current popular formulations would have us believe. As Spiritual Leaders, we are not

---

23. Richmond, *Piaget*, 190.

24. After all, a crisis is only a crisis because it demands the use of our non-dominant sides. Should a situation arise that calls solely on our strengths, it is most likely that the ease with which we would navigate would preclude naming it a crisis.

simply ministers, or educators, or scholars, or counselors. By the very nature of the intimate depths we must touch in our clients, students, readers, or congregants (whether it be conscious or non-conscious action), we have no recourse but to be superbly responsible and uniquely congruent as we attempt to bring light to the quest for God. As such, my conception of true Spiritual Leadership evokes the image of one of the most encompassing, complex, and taxing professions of our day. A true Spiritual Leader, then, is an educator, a minister, a scholar, a counselor, a friend, and a disciple: all of these roles, all at once, all of the time. Spiritual Leadership is one of the last bastions of co-natural knowledge: the type of knowledge that cannot be passed on unless it is deeply believed and faithfully lived. It is through this deep belief, this faithful living, that I believe Spiritual Leaders learn to make meaning; and the meanings themselves are the holy beacons that will light the path of clients, as they struggle and yearn to more clearly see.

Prologue Extended

OUR DISCUSSION THROUGHOUT THESE pages has focused on human evolution and Emergence, and how this evolution can be strengthened and furthered by the actions of adept, prayerful, and knowledgeable Spiritual Leaders. I have argued that human growth is an Emerging evolution of consciousness which gives rise to meaning-making and spirituality. I have described a comprehensive framework within which this evolution can be elegantly portrayed and understood. In addition, I presented this framework as the founding platform upon which Spiritual Leaders can approach their clients. As such, Spiritual Leaders humbly accompany clients through the process of Emergence by co-constructing with the client a culture of embeddedness. The culture is created through an unwavering commitment to the person of the client (as seen through the lens of constructivist-developmentalism) and not through a staunch defense of the system within which the Spiritual Leader functions. Taken together, these two arguments challenge the Church to redefine its role and its place in society, in education, and in the world at large. Thus, I believe that the cultural repudiation of Spiritual Leaders can be curbed and transformed into a powerful force for human evolution.

It is my belief that this repudiation, which is commonly observed in Western culture, stems from an angered loss of trust in the institution of Spiritual Leadership. In other words, many voices in today's culture are crying out that they feel betrayed by the institution of Spiritual Leadership, because this Leadership has proven to be a very negative and confusing force in their lives. Too often for my own comfort, I have come face-to-face with stories in which clients have felt betrayed, coerced, and even abused by the attitudes and biases of Spiritual Leaders. The gradual distancing of society from the influences of Spiritual Leadership is making itself felt very strongly, from coast to coast, in our evolving and growing country. No longer are the old standards and adages sufficient to lead the complex population through the labyrinth that is their daily experience. No longer do magical stories and heart-warming parables carry spirit-altering effects within the souls of a cynical and guarded society. No longer do scripted answers and platitudes hold comfort for a dynamic, intelligent, educated, and autonomous people. Our culture is sending clear messages of what it needs to rectify this downward spiral of experience and openness: it needs a transformation in the consciousness of Spiritual Leadership.

In the first prologue of this work, I asked a couple of questions: can we redefine the role of Spiritual Leaders in order to develop and accept a founding epistemology that transcends and unites views and cultures that have traditionally pitted us against one another? Can we redefine the role for Spiritual Leaders in order to set the basis for a Christian culture that is built upon concern for each individual, and not upon concern for the propagation of a traditional system? It is my belief that, in overlooking these pressing issues, we create a culture of Spiritual Leadership that denies the beauty and value of each member of humanity. It is my belief that, in staunchly defending Spiritual Leadership in the form in which it has always existed, we denigrate the evolutionary force through which humanity has been created to progress. It is my belief that in eclipsing our vision of the person for the comfort of a plush and sedentary epistemology, we demean Yahweh and His Holy Spirit by representing them as partisan, culturally-embedded, narrow-minded and even political. As such, I believe that it is in invoking the Name of Yahweh toward non-transformational or partisan ends, that we truly take it in vain.

Can Spiritual Leadership evolve the strength of consciousness necessary to transform its goals from compliance and obedience to transformation and growth? Can Spiritual Leadership evolve the impetus toward life that would transform its static and self-righteous stance into a dynamic and client-centered stance? Can Spiritual Leadership evolve the security of spirit to transform itself from the Guardian of God to the Child of God? Can Spiritual Leadership find the groundedness within its evolution to transform its focus from the letter of the Law to the Christ-like Spirit of the Law? Can Spiritual Leadership evolve the ability to transcend the distinctions of 'conservative' or 'liberal', and embrace an epistemology of spirituality, meaning, evolution, and coherence? Can Spiritual Leadership evolve the vision of spirit to shift its energy from condemning the incompleteness of other cultures to examining the incompleteness of its own?

The answers to these questions are the future of the work presented in these pages. I believe that the institution of Spiritual Leadership is itself undergoing an evolutionary transition. Just as the person's path to transformation involves the weathering and accommodation of opposition, so Spiritual Leadership stands at the threshold of transformation as it finds opposition in the voice of its vulnerable and innocent clients. It is the purpose of my research to be an encouraging and fearless voice that walks compassionately next to the groaning and re-equilibrating Leadership, as it transforms itself into the powerful instrument God has decreed it to be. I believe that at the end of this challenge, should Spiritual Leaders choose to take it on, lies a world in which Spiritual Leadership returns to a place of trust and ascendancy in the daily struggles of culture and of humanity.

Just as the story of the Pentateuch ends with Moses, standing on a distant hill, watching as the future of his people lay uncertain before their feet, so the story of the evolution of Spiritual Leadership lay before us as an unfinished and on-going work. As such, we are truly at the beginning of this epic quest. Thus, the end of the Pentateuch tells us clearly that God has ordered the created universe such that we will never be released from the mission and challenge to continually learn to see.

Bibliography

Alexander, T. Desmond. *From Paradise to the Promised Land*. Grand Rapids: Baker, 1995.
Alt, Albrecht. *Essays on Old Testament History and Religion*. Garden City, NY: Doubleday, 1968.
Antony, D. John. *Psychotherapies in Counseling*. Tamilnadu, India: Anugraha, 2003.
———. *Skills in Counseling*. Tamilnadu, India: Anugraha, 1995.
Aristotle. *Nichomachean Ethics*. Translated by D. Ross. Oxford: Oxford University Press, 1980.
Bacal, Howard, and Kenneth Newman. *Theories of Object Relations: Bridges to Self-Psychology*. New York: Columbia University Press, 1990.
Barnet, Ann, and Richard Barnet. *The Youngest Minds: Parenting and Genetic Inheritance in the Development of Intellect and Emotion*. New York: Touchstone, 1998.
Bellous, Joyce. E. *Educating Faith: An Approach to Spiritual Formation*. Toronto: Clements, 2006.
Benner, David. *Strategic Pastoral Counseling*. Grand Rapids: Baker, 1992.
Bloom, Howard. *Exodus*. New Haven: Chelsea House, 1987.
Boden, Margaret. *Piaget*. London: Fontana, 1979.
Bollas, Christopher. *The Shadow of the Object*. New York: Norton, 1993.
Bonhoeffer, Dietrich. *Letters and Papers from Prison*. New York: Touchstone, 1953.
Bowlby, John. *Attachment*. New York: Basic Books, 1969.
Brown, A. L. *On Hegel*. Belmont, CA: Wadsworth, 2001.
Eliot, George. *Middlemarch*. Oxford: Oxford University Press, 1998.
Erikson, Erick. *The Erik Erickson Reader*, edited by R. Coles. New York: Norton, 2000.
Capps, Donald. *Agents of Hope*. Minneapolis: Fortress, 1995.
———. *Living Stories: Pastoral Care in a Congregational Context*. Minneapolis: Fortress, 1997.
Coles, Robert. *The Moral Life of Children*. Boston: Houghton Mifflin, 1986.
Clines, David. *The Theme of the Pentateuch*. Sheffield, England: University of Sheffield Press, 1978.
David, Catherine, et al. *Conversations about the End of Time*. London, England: Penguin, 1999.
Dozeman, Thomas. *God At War: Power in the Exodus Tradition*. Oxford: Oxford University Press, 1996.
Erickson, Erick. *Childhood and Society*. New York: Norton, 1968.
Eriksen, Karen. "Toward a Constructivist and Developmental Identity for the Counseling Profession." In JCD, September 30, 1999, http://www.media-server.amazon.com/exec/drm/amzproxy.cgi, accessed on September 18, 2005.
Fowler, James. *Stages of Faith: The Psychology of Human Development and the Quest for Meaning*. San Francisco: Harper Collins, 1981.

Frankl, Victor. *Man's Search for Meaning.* New York: Pocket Books, 1963.
Freud, Sigmund. *Basic Writings of Sigmund Freud.* Translated by A. Brill. New York: Random House, 1995.
Gagnon, George, and Michelle Collay. *Designing for Learning: Six Elements in Constructivist Classroom.* Thousand Oaks, CA: Corwin, 2001.
Gardner, Howard. *Frames of Mind: The Theory of Multiple Intelligences.* New York: Basic Books, 2004.
———. *Multiple Intelligences: The Theory in Practice, A Reader.* New York: Basic Book, 1993.
Gendlin, Eugene. *Focusing.* New York: Bantam, 1979.
Gertoux, Gerard. *The Name of God Yehowah Pronounced as It Is Written.* New York: University of America Press, 2002.
Goldberg, Carl. *Speaking with the Devil: Exploring Senseless Acts of Evil.* New York: Penguin, 1996.
Goleman, Daniel. *Emotional Intelligence.* New York: Bantam, 1995.
Greene, Brian. *The Fabric of the Cosmos.* New York: Random House, 2003.
Hawking, Stephen. *A Brief History of Time.* New York: Bantam, 1988.
Hegel, Georg. Wilhelm. *The Phenomenology of Mind.* Translated by J. Bailie. New York: Harper & Row, 1967.
Heiss, Robert. *Hegel, Kierkegaard, Marx: Three Great Philosophers Whose Ideas Changed the Course of Civilization.* Berlin, Germany: Delacourte, 1963.
Humphreys, Colin. *Miracles of Exodus: A Scientist's Discovery.* San Francisco: HarperSanFransisco, 2003.
Kegan, Robert. *The Evolving Self.* Cambridge, Massachusetts: Harvard University Press, 1982.
———. *In Over Our Heads: The Mental Demands of Modern Life.* Cambridge, MA: Harvard University Press, 1994.
Kegan Robert., and Lisa Lahey. *How the Way We Talk Can Change the Way We Work.* San Francisco: Jossey-Bass, 2001.
Kierkegaard, Soren. *The Journal of Kierkegaard.* Translated by A. Dru. New York: Harper, 1959.
Knight, George. *Theology as Narrative.* Edinburgh, Scotland: Handsel, 1976.
Kohlberg, Lawrence. *Moral Stages: A Current Formulation and a Response to Critics.* Basel, Swizterland: Karger, 1983.
———. *The Adolescent as a Philosopher.* New York: Norton, 1972.
Kohut, Heinz. *The Analysis of Self.* New York: International Universities Press, 1971.
Krause, Elizabeth. *The Metaphysics of Experience: A Companion to Whitehead's Process and Reality.* New York: Fondham University Press, 1998.
Lande, Nathaniel., and Afton Slade. *Stages: Understanding How You Make Moral Decisions.* San Francisco: Harper & Row, 1979.
Lefebvre, Henri. *Dialectical Materialism.* London: Jonathan Cape, 1968.
Levinson, Bernard. *Deutoronomy and the Hermeneutics of Legal Innovation.* Oxford: Oxford University Press, 1997.
Lonergan, Bernard. *Method in Theology.* New York: Herder and Herder, 1972.
———. *Insight: A Study of Human Understanding.* San Francisco: Harper & Row, 1958.
Mackie, Marlene. *Constructing Men and Women.* Toronto: Holt, Rinehart, and Winston, 1987.

Malone, Patrick, and Thomas Malone. *The Windows of Experience: Moving Beyond Recovery to Wholeness.* New York: Simon & Schuster, 1992.
Mann, Thomas. *The Book of Torah.* Atlanta: John Knox, 1971.
Marcuse, Herbert. *Studies in Critical Philosophy.* Boston: Beacon, 1972.
Marmorstein, Arthur. *The Old Rabbinic Doctrine of God.* London: Oxford University Press, 1927.
Meyer, Carol. *The Message of Exodus.* Minneapolis: Augsburg, 1983.
Misak, Cheryl. *Truth and the End of Enquiry,* Oxford: Oxford Philosophical Monographs, 2004.
Miller, Jean. B. *Toward a New Psychology of Women.* Boston: Beacon, 1976.
Moberly, R. *The Old Testament of the Old Testament.* Minneapolis: Fortress, 1992.
Moody, Harry. *The Five Stages of the Soul.* New York: Anchor, 1997.
Myers, David. *Psychology.* New York: Worth, 1984.
Neuser, Jacob. *Torah.* Philadelphia: Fortress, 1985.
Nichols, Michael. *The Lost Art of Listening.* New York: Guileford, 1995.
Parke-Taylor, Geoffrey. *Yahweh: The Divine Name in the Bible.* Waterloo, ON: Wilfred Laurier University Press, 1975.
Paul, Robert. *Moses and Civilization.* New Haven: Yale University Press, 1996.
Peck, M. Scott. *The Road Less Traveled and Beyond.* New York: Simon & Schuster, 1997.
———. *The Road Less Traveled.* New York: Touchstone, 1978.
———. *The Different Drum.* New York: Touchstone, 1987.
Peirce, Charles S., *Collected Papers of Charles Sanders Peirce,* vols. 1–6, 1931–1935, edited by Charles Hartshorne and Paul Weiss. Vols. 7–8, edited by Arthur W. Burks. Cambridge, MA: Harvard University Press, 1958.
Perry, William. *Forms of Intellectual and Ethical Development in the College Years.* New York: Holt, Rinehart, and Winston, 1970.
Piaget, Jean. *The Constructions of Reality in the Child.* New York: Basic Books, 1954.
Propp, William. *Exodus 1–18.* New York: Doubleday, 1998.
Richmond, Peter, G. *An Introduction to Piaget.* New York: Basic Books, 1970.
Rogers, Carl. *Client-Centered Therapy.* Boston: Houghton Mifflin, 1961.
Rose, Frank, and Bob Maginel. *The Joy of Spiritual Growth.* West Chester, PA: Swedenborg Foundation, 1999.
Roth, Ron. *Prayer and the Five Stages of Healing.* Carlsbad, CA: Hay House, 1999.
Sanford, John. *The Man Who Wrestled With God.* New York: Paulist, 1974.
Scruton, Roger, et al. *German Philosophers: Kant, Hegel, Schopenhauer, Nietzsche.* Oxford: Oxford University Press, 1983.
Seobock, John. *Signs.* New York: Harper, 1988.
Smith, William. *Belief and History.* Charlottesville, VA: University Press of Virginia, 1977.
Steffe, Leslie, and Jerry Gale. *Constructivism in Education.* Hillsdale, NJ: Lawrence Erlbaum, 1995.
Stern, Daniel. *Diary of a Baby.* New York: Basic Books, 1990.
Stiebing, William. *Out of the Desert? Archeology and the Exodus.* Buffalo: Prometheus, 1989.
Sullivan, Harold. S. *The Interpersonal Theory of Psychiatry.* New York, Norton, 1953.
Swimme, Brian and Thomas Berry. *The Universe Story.* San Francisco: HarperSanFrancisco, 1992.
Szasz, Thomas. *The Myth of Mental Illness.* New York: Harper, 1961.

Teilhard de Chardin, Pierre. *The Phenomenon of Man*. New York: Harper & Row, 1955.

Tillich, Paul. *Dynamics of Faith*. New York: Harper & Row, 1957.

Whitehead. Alfred. N. *Process and Reality*, edited by D. Griffin and D. Sherburne. New York: Free Press, 1978.

Winnicott, Donald. *The Maturational Processes and the Facilitating Environment*. New York: International University Press, 1982.

Wolterstorff, Nicholas. *John Locke and the Ethics of Belief*. Cambridge: Cambridge University Press, 1996.

———. *Reason Within the Bounds of Religion*. Lanham, MD: Rowman & Littlefield, 1997.

Yerushalma, Yosef. *Freud's Moses*. New Haven: Yale University Press, 1991.

Zohar, Danah and Ian Marshall. *Spiritual Intelligence: The Ultimate Intelligence*. London: Bloomsbury, 2000.

www.ingramcontent.com/pod-product-compliance
Lightning Source LLC
Chambersburg PA
CBHW071230170426
43191CB00032B/1222